PENG

91 PREDICTIONS

Greenstone Lobo worked as a human resource professional before turning into a full-time astrologer in 2019. He has tested and practised the principles of astrology in the corporate environment for over twenty-five years. He is credited with creating an entirely new system of astrology, with a 16-planet methodology, based on original research and a scientific approach. His unique calculator considers the significance of the planets Uranus, Neptune and most importantly, Pluto—besides three new planetoids—X, Y, and Z. Greenstone correctly predicted the winners of three consecutive Cricket World Cups in 2011, 2015, and 2019.

He also predicted the results of the general elections in India three times, consecutively, in 2009, 2014, and 2019. The astrologer has been teaching his 16-Planet-Scientific-Astrology course both online and offline for several years. He has trained over a thousand students, some of whom are now practising astrologers.

He has a regular column 'Octozone' on sports astrology, in the Indian daily, *DNA*, since 2008. He was also a columnist for *Anandabazar Patrika* and Sportskeeda.com. His opinions, advisory columns, predictions, and articles have appeared in the *Times of India*, *Mumbai Mirror*, *The Telegraph*, *Life Positive* and *Sangbad Pratidin*. He has also appeared on RadioCity, Radio One, Radio Mirchi and KCOR (USA). His two published books are—*What is Your True Zodiac Sign? and Howzzat: 50 Predictions on Indian Cricket You Won't Believe*.

Greenstone was honoured with the WOW Award for his extraordinary contribution to the field of astrology in 2019. He has clients all across the globe and is a regular visiting astrologer at Illuminations, Dubai.

Website: https://greenstonelobo.com/
Online astrology course: https://www.16planetastrology.com/
Facebook: https://www.facebook.com/ScientificAstrologer/
Twitter: @GreenstoneLobo

91
PREDICTIONS

THE FATE OF THE WORLD
AND ITS PEOPLE IN
THE NEXT HALF-CENTURY

GREENSTONE
LOBO

PENGUIN BOOKS

An imprint of Penguin Random House

PENGUIN BOOKS

USA | Canada | UK | Ireland | Australia
New Zealand | India | South Africa | China

Penguin Books is part of the Penguin Random House group of companies
whose addresses can be found at global.penguinrandomhouse.com

Published by Penguin Random House India Pvt. Ltd
4th Floor, Capital Tower 1, MG Road,
Gurugram 122 002, Haryana, India

| Penguin
Random House
India

First published by Westland Publication Private Limited in 2021
This edition published in Penguin Books by Penguin Random House India in 2023

10 9 8 7 6 5 4 3 2 1

ISBN 9780143459149

Typeset by New Media Line Creation
Printed at Replika Press Pvt. Ltd, India

www.penguin.co.in

MIX
Paper from
responsible sources
FSC® C016779

To the genius scientist who will restore Pluto's dignity, honour and its rightful place as a planet in the solar system.

Contents

Introduction

People often ask me why I am known as a 'scientific astrologer' when it is, actually, a contradiction in terms, since no scientist believes in astrology, and astrology itself is 'poppycock', used by charlatans and mountebanks to rob gullible or mentally vulnerable people. They believe astrology has no scientific basis—it isn't even formally recognised as an academic subject worthy of study or exploration.

Through this book my intention is to bust these myths. I wish to exhibit that astrology is a science, a subject worthy of attention, exploration, serious study and application. And I will prove it using my own methodology, based on approximately thirty years of primary research, experimentation and deductions. This methodology is somewhat different from the Vedic or Western systems which have been used in predictive astrology for ages.

Why is astrology a science? Because there is empirical evidence to prove it works, and it works every time, regardless of variables, as in any scientific experiment. Yes, there may be missing links, as there are in any branch of science—take the Periodic Table, for instance—but those gaps can be, and may well be, filled some day. In this book we shall see some glimpses of the application of astrology as a science.

I also believe that science and astrology or science and religion are not opposites but complements or correlatives. They need each other to make a composite whole.

Just as the planets in our solar system have physical and chemical properties, they have astrological properties as well. These properties affect each person and all that happens in the world. This is the basic premise of astrology. Listing these properties and understanding their impact is imperative. Our exploration and astrological journey begins from here.

And how am I going to prove that astrology is a science? Well, by using the same formula that science uses. Extrapolation. In science, first, on the basis of certain assumptions and a few facts, we form a hypothesis. Then, with various examples, we prove that the assumptions are correct and any deviation or exception simply proves the rule. Thus, supported by enough data, it becomes a theory.

In this book I'll talk about various such hypotheses in astrology and show how they have manifested themselves in the past. Later, we will extrapolate from the past and use the results to predict the future. We won't simply do one or two but 91 forecasts.

Join the ride!

Everything Comes in Cycles

By March 2020, the belief that we were in the midst of something very unusual started sinking in. People everywhere were wearing masks. There was social distancing—we were supposed to stay away from one another. Jokes about how you had no choice but to be with and love your own spouse went the rounds. Large businesses and malls shut down, some small businesses thrived, people lost their jobs. You now realised what true essentials were. There was panic and uncertainty, a true VUCA moment I used to talk about in my corporate leadership programmes—volatility, uncertainty, complexity and ambiguity. You were not sure about how the next month, or even the following week, would unfold. Some people said it was almost like living during war times. The only difference was that here you were dealing with an unknown, unseen enemy.

Is it really true that something like this has never happened before? Think again. Something very similar did occur a hundred years ago. Almost 99.9 per cent of the world's current population wasn't even born a hundred years ago, and hence we do not remember this extraordinary event. During 1918–1920, millions of people were infected with the Spanish Flu. Almost fifteen million people died in India alone. You can see images of those times on the internet. People wore masks, were quarantined, and millions died due to lack of medical facilities or a cure. And yes, something similar will happen even in the future with a frequency we should be able to calculate.

Everything comes in cycles. Events repeat themselves in a country's economy too. Economists talk about recurring peaks, troughs and plateaus associated with economic cycles and use different theories to explain these spikes and slumps. As an astrologer I was supposed to know this was coming. I didn't. I don't have an excuse. However, just like engineers have different specialities—civil, nuclear, automobile, software and so on—astrologers also specialise in particular, narrow fields. While there is a common interest in the details of human life, such as career, health, wealth and relationships, some of us venture beyond and explore other applications of astrology like political, financial and sports events. Astrologers also predict weather, climate changes and natural disasters such as earthquakes. Collectively, this is called 'mundane astrology'. You need a deep interest and a good amount of data to learn and then predict events connected to these cases.

My interest lies mainly in sports astrology. As an eleven-year-old, in 1983, I saw Kapil Dev and his team lift the Cricket World Cup trophy. This piqued my interest in sports, particularly cricket. I picked up my first book on astrology in 1986, at the age of fourteen. I read almost a hundred books on astrology over the next five years. During the 1996 Cricket World Cup, I wondered if an event as unpredictable as sports can be predicted. After a thorough study of mundane astrology, specifically sports astrology, spanning a decade-and-a-half, in 2011, I predicted that Mahendra Singh Dhoni would lead India to victory in the next World Cup.[1]

Over the years I have made similar predictions about football, tennis and badminton. I've also indulged in political astrology, where my predictions have been about real people and interesting events. These predictions have been about real people and interesting events. The weather and natural disasters didn't interest me too much, and so I didn't make any effort to

[1]   Greenstone Lobo, 'Whose Stars Are Shining Brightest?' *DNA*, 21 March 2011, https://www.dnaindia.com/sports/comment-whose-stars-are-shining-brightest-1522344.

study them. A pandemic, which is classified under 'mundane' astrology, was the last thing on my mind.

If I say I had a premonition that there would be a pandemic, it may sound dubious since I cannot substantiate it with a newspaper article or an internet blog. But I expected 'death' to be a big theme in 2020 and wrote a Facebook post[2] on it in the first week of January 2020. Since I was not studying the field, I wasn't sure what would trigger these deaths and how. After the pandemic hit the world and changed routine life and its dynamics completely, it prompted me to look at the future by revisiting the past.

I knew about the astrological significance of the planet Pluto and the grand scale on which it can operate. However, I realised the full impact of its movement only after the event had already taken place. Now I realise it has a clear connection to the Spanish flu that happened a hundred years ago. Since I haven't studied it earlier, I consider it is my duty now to analyse the past in greater detail so that we can envision an accurate future for all of us. And we will probably be better prepared the next time round. As I mentioned earlier, everything comes in cycles.

---

[2]   https://www.facebook.com/permalink.php?story_fbid=10218276060926131&id=1629143959

Pluto Creates Cycles

I have read over four hundred books on astrology by Indian and Western astrologers. Yet, explanations offered about the lives of some well-known people remain unclear. Why was Hitler a Nazi? Which planet made Mahatma Gandhi a huge national leader? Why was (or wasn't) Mata Hari involved in espionage?

The quest to find answers to these and several other such questions led me on a Maharishi Parashar[3] was one of the well-known sages of ancient India. He is called a 'maharishi', which translates as 'great seer'. He was the great-grandfather of both the Kauravas and the Pandavas, the two warring factions in the Mahabharata. That means he lived around 3000 BC. He has been credited as the author of many ancient texts. One of them is the *Brihat Parashara Hora Shastra*, the most ancient treatise on astrology. He can be called the 'Father of Indian Astrology'.

The Vedic and the Western astrology systems rely on some of the planets in the solar system and their positions in different 'houses' or the zodiac signs in a person's birth chart, to make their predictions. The real trouble begins when you plot all the zodiac signs against their supposed ruling planets. The Indian system of astrology uses only five planets in its analyses—just five planets to describe twelve zodiac signs! And the Sun and the Moon are assigned as rulers of two zodiac signs—Leo and Cancer. To me, it was obvious that twelve zodiac signs must have twelve different ruling planets, but there were only eight in the solar system (barring Earth).

---

[3] Yogesh Sharma, 'Rishi Parashar', *Speakingtree.in*, 1 May 2015, https://www.speakingtree.in/blog/rishi-parashara.

It is interesting to note that Indian astrologers today do not use heavenly bodies beyond Saturn in their astrological analysis. The reason given is that these bodies are too far away from Earth to impact human beings. Another rebuttal to their significance is that our Vedic texts do not talk about these bodies. Maharshi Parashar has mentioned about seven upagrahas beyond Saturn—Varuna, Yama, Prajapati, Indra, Kuber, Isan and Vayu[4]. With modern telescopes, we now know that there are three planets beyond Saturn—Uranus, Neptune and Pluto—and probably some more which the astronomers have not yet discovered. The seer, though, could 'see' them without any apparatus.

In the table here, you will see that the Indian and the Western systems differ in assigning planets to certain zodiac signs.

Zodiac sign	Planet assigned according to Indian astrology	Planet assigned according to Western astrology	Is there an anomaly here?
Aries	Mars	Mars	
Taurus	Venus	Venus	Venus also rules Libra. How can one planet rule two zodiac signs?
Gemini	Mercury	Mercury	Mercury also rules Virgo.
Cancer	Moon	Moon	Moon is not a planet.

---

[4] *Brihat Parashara Hora Shastra*, chapter 3, verses 61–64.

Leo	Sun	Sun	Sun is not a planet.
Virgo	Mercury	Mercury/ Chiron (some astrologers)	Is it Chiron for sure?
Libra	Venus	Venus	Venus also rules Taurus.
Scorpio	Mars	Pluto	
Sagittarius	Jupiter	Jupiter	
Capricorn	Saturn	Saturn	
Aquarius	Saturn	Uranus	
Pisces	Jupiter	Neptune	

So, which bodies should be included in the analysis? The simple answer is, if there are twelve zodiac signs, then there should be twelve planets ruling them.

It took me about twenty-five years of research to create my own unique methodology of practising astrology. This is my contribution to astrology. In this methodology I use all the eight planets, excluding Earth, as we are looking at things geocentrically, and including Pluto, the Sun and the Moon, Chiron and, additionally, three more planetoids. These three planetoids are called centaurs by International Astronomical Union (IAU) and their assigned codes are 2007 RH283, 1999 JV127 and 2008 FC76. I call these bodies Planet-X, Planet-Y and Planet-Z, for the sake of simplicity.

In astrology, each zodiac sign is assigned a ruling planet. The fiery and aggressive Aries is ruled by the energetic Mars, the love-struck Libra is ruled by the beautiful Venus, and the talkative Gemini is ruled by Mercury. Then which planet rules the hypnotic Scorpio? Well, it is the deep Pluto. Over a period of time, I realised that this was a huge anomaly in the Indian system of astrology. Greek mythology has extraordinary descriptions of Uranus, Neptune and Pluto. The Greek god Hades is called Pluto in Roman mythology.[5] Hades is the lord of the underworld and the god of death.

Pluto takes 256 years to go around the Sun once. Compare that with Jupiter, which takes twelve years, or Saturn which takes thirty years. Perhaps the length of time a planet takes to circumnavigate the Sun has astrological significance. The shape and size of a planet, perhaps, don't really matter. What matters is the distance from the Sun. Since Pluto comes into a strong position less frequently, it probably creates only a handful of great people when it does.

Since thousands of years, in every mythology and civilisation, be it Greek, Roman or Chinese, the heavenly bodies have always been associated with religion. An interesting question here may be, did the astrological deductions or associations come first or was it religion? While you still think about this question, I have another one for you—who are the most popular gods in India? Perhaps, Krishna, Shiva and Ganesha. It is really surprising that none of these three gods is associated with any zodiac sign. What percentage of people visit Buddh, Shukra or Shani temples compared to one dedicated to Shiva or Ganesha?

If I need to share one important learning from my thirty years of study, it is that the most powerful planet in this universe is—Pluto! Pluto's transit into any zodiac sign and its period of stay there is marked by a huge set of unique events and a major transition. Pluto rules the entire birth–death cycle.[6] It resonates with the path of rebirth–renewal–reset. It is responsible for

---

[5]   'Hades', *Encyclopaedia Britannica*, https://www.britannica.com/topic/Hades-Greek-mythology.

[6]   'Pluto', *Tarot.com*, 10 September 2019, https://www.tarot.com/astrology/planets/pluto.

upheavals, wars, destructions and transformations. Since Pluto is the ruling planet of their zodiac, Scorpios are transformative, strong, deep and very powerful.

My fascination for Pluto made me look for a god in Indian mythology who would reflect the qualities associated with this powerful planet. I didn't have to struggle much. Pluto is Shiva. Look at all the characteristics of Pluto and the traits associated with Shiva. Our ancestors knew about Pluto and what it stood for—birth, destruction, regeneration, reset, renewal. Everything that Shiva stands for.

Whenever I found a horoscope I couldn't explain using the traditional planets, I would assume that one of these 'missing' planets must be ruling the zodiac signs of the horoscope. For instance, while I could find out the astrological reason for why Amitabh Bachchan had met with an accident while filming *Coolie*, or why he had gone bankrupt, I couldn't explain why he became a legendary actor or which planet was responsible for his extraordinary comeback. I was sure one of the 'yet-to-be-discovered' planets was responsible for those happenings and it was likely placed in a strategic position in his birth chart. I was also sure that one of the missing planets was the ruler of one of the four zodiac signs of Taurus, Virgo, Leo or Cancer.

I was sure there was some Planet-X and some Planet-Y ruling Taurus and Virgo. If we discovered these two, many unanswered questions would be resolved. Perhaps the heavenly bodies were still within IAU's reach and had even been identified, but didn't fall in their definition of planets, and probably would be called by some other name rather than planets. But they were surely there somewhere. I just needed to find them. I was also wondering if Chiron was actually the true ruler of Cancer and not Virgo.

The following table shows what I consider to be the true rulers of the various zodiac signs and also some of the keywords connected to the planets. When a planet is positively placed, it shows positive manifestations in the areas connected to it. When it is placed negatively in a zodiac sign, it creates the opposite impact. While planets like Mercury, Venus and Mars largely impact our persona, those at a further distance influence other sectors connected to them.

Zodiac sign	Ruler	Keywords
Aries	Mars	Energy, passion, courage, valour, stamina
Taurus	Planet-X	Wealth, materialistic success, money in all forms, luxury, business
Gemini	Mercury	Communication, ideas, intelligence, motion, fun
Cancer	Chiron	Family, children, real estate, land, food, agriculture, vehicles, motherland
Leo	Planet-Z	Showbiz, media, beauty, arts, entertainment, technology, advisory
Virgo	Planet-Y	Design, data, engineering, technology, process, efficiency, granular
Libra	Venus	Arts, beauty, love, romance, relationships
Scorpio	Pluto	Birth–death cycle, re-engineering, renewal, reset, upheavals, transformation
Sagittarius	Jupiter	Knowledge, teaching, travels, expansion, spirituality, luck factor
Capricorn	Saturn	Ambition, authority, status, hardships, obstacles, pessimism
Aquarius	Uranus	Technology, unorthodox, progressive, innovation, sudden, independent
Pisces	Neptune	Mythical, magical, maya, sea, wisdom, spirituality, confusion, tragedy

The Supporting Cast—Uranus, Neptune and Planet-X

Brahma, Vishnu and Mahesh—the Trimurti—are amongst the most popular gods in India. It's amazing how the descriptions of these three tie in with the qualities of Uranus, Neptune and Pluto.

Brahma is the Creator, Vishnu is the Preserver and Mahesh is the Destroyer. I would like to use the word Destroyer in a positive sense here. Mahesh destroys to re-create. People who invent or create something have Pluto in a very strong position in their birth chart. A person who enhances something that already exists has Uranus in a strong position. The Lumière brothers, Auguste and Louis, who invented the cinema, had Pluto in the strongest position in their birth charts; for Walt Disney, the innovative animator, it was Uranus. Bill Gates, pioneer in his field, has Pluto in the strongest position, and so did Steve Jobs; Larry Page and Sergey Brin, the technology superstars, have a well-placed Uranus.

I would equate Brahma with Uranus. After Shiva's role is over, Brahma takes over. Uranus stands for the disruption of the old order. Creation and innovation are two extremely different dimensions ruled by Pluto and Uranus, respectively. Creation is bringing in something that never existed before. Innovation is improving something which already exists. Any work that is unorthodox, progressive and different can be attributed to Uranus. But do remember that an innovation can be brought about only in something that already exists. Pluto gives birth to something, Uranus innovates and improvises on that.

So what does Neptune do then? Or what is the role of Vishnu?

Vishnu's role goes beyond preservation. Yes, some of the greatest achievements and legacies in the world that have enduring power always have the stamp of Neptune. Most of the biggest monuments of the world that have stood the test of time were built during the stronger transits of Neptune. The rebuilding of the city of Paris, including the Eiffel Tower, also happened during strong Neptune transit.

The Taj Mahal was created when Neptune was in the deepest exaltation. It has an alluring, ethereal beauty. When you look at the Taj Mahal, you feel it is magic. It looks so surreal that it almost feels like an illusion. Neptune rules maya or illusion. The film industry is one of the greatest products of Neptune. Also called 'mayanagari' (the city of illusions), it can be ascribed to the positive influences of Neptune. No surprise then that some of the greatest actors in the world have Neptune in the strongest position in their birth charts, be it Marlon Brando, Shah Rukh Khan or Brad Pitt.

The Taj Mahal is not just a monument, but also a tomb. It is a symbol of beauty, but also of tragedy. The greatest tragedies in the world have also occurred during the times when Neptune is in a strong position. Neptune also rules water. The biggest tragedies related to water can be pinned on Neptune—be it tsunamis, the sinking of the Titanic or other such major fatal accidents.

Neptune also creates confusion in its negative avatar. If there is any situation in the world where commotion or confusion rules, we can be sure it has been created because of Neptune. Even in the world of finance, where everything is based on numbers and data, when Neptune enters a weak position, it can create confusion or even carelessness and there could be a commotion in the market.

One of the most popular Indian gods is the elephant god

Ganesha. Ganesha is the remover of obstacles and provider of achievements and success, one whose blessings are sought before you start a project. He is correlated to Planet-X, the true ruler of the zodiac sign of Taurus. In a result-oriented world, you can term something as a success or an achievement if there is a positive financial outcome. Planet-X stands for everything materialistic, money in all its forms, financial matters, businesses, wealth in any form and everything related to monetary transactions.

While Pluto takes 256 years for a revolution, Planet-X takes about sixty-four years, Uranus takes eighty-four years and Neptune takes 162 years for one revolution. So, while Pluto is in a zodiac sign creating something new in its positive avatar, Neptune could be preserving something already created, Uranus could be improving it further, while Planet-X could be influencing some form of wealth in people's lives. All of this could be happening simultaneously at any point of time, because all the planets play their part in a birth chart or a person's life— depending on their positive or negative influences at that time.

Planets in a negative transit could also be destroying something. Neptune could be creating a tragedy or confusion and Uranus could be creating a volatile situation somewhere. That is the interesting interplay of planetary positions.

Zero–10–25 Degrees of Separation

'There are hundreds of people born in a day. There could be many born on the day Sachin Tendulkar was born. Then why didn't they all become greats?' Derek Abraham, my friend and my sounding board, asked me. I replied, 'Let's try to verify this.'

Sachin Tendulkar was born in Nirmal Nursing Home, Dadar on 24 April 1973.7 On 20 April 2013, Derek visited this nursing home and managed to lay his hands on the register where Sachin's birth was recorded. Derek was amused, 'He was the only child to be born that day. Probably indicates why he was special.'

Gaurav Kapur and his team visited the hospital where Sunil Gavaskar, the legendary Indian cricketer, was born—Purandare's Hospital near Chowpatty, Mumbai. Interestingly, Gavaskar was the only child born on the 10 July 1949. There were many children born on the next day8. But he was the only one on that day.

This question always used to haunt me—what makes some people great and the rest of us ordinary? By 'great' I mean an extraordinary achiever in any field or domain and the world's most celebrated in that area, like Amitabh Bachchan, Muhammad Ali, Roger Federer, Bill Gates, Stephen Hawking, J.K. Rowling, to name a few.

---

[7]   Derek Abraham, 'Sachin Tendulkar: The multi-million dollar baby', *DNA*, 24 April 2014, https://www.dnaindia.com/sports/report-sachin-tendulkar-the-multi-million-dollar-baby-1826338.

[8]   Interview with Gaurav Kapur on *Breakfast for Champions*, 'Sunil Gavaskar: Sunny's greatest cricketing memories!' 18 August 2017, https://www.youtube.com/watch?v=rzh0sHUM_yI&t=688s.

Malcolm Gladwell, in his book *Outliers*, suggested that greats were born during particular months of the year. He was correct to some extent.

The birthdays of some of the greatest people in the world are grouped together and they were born during specific periods. Is it a coincidence that the year 1946 produced three American presidents who, between them, served five presidential terms? George W. Bush, Bill Clinton and Donald Trump were all born in the same year—1946. And it's no coincidence either that the greatest of superstars who ruled Indian cinema in different decades—Amitabh Bachchan, Jitendra and Rajesh Khanna—were all born in the same year—1942. Again, it's no coincidence that the three superstar Khans—Shah Rukh, Salman and Aamir—were all born in the same year—1965. You can add another Khan—Farah Khan—to the list. And Sooraj Barjatya, too, if you want.

It is astonishing that the greatest superstars of cricket, football and tennis during the 2000s were born on the same year—1981—M.S. Dhoni, Iker Casillas and Roger Federer. The next set of superstars in the respective games were born in either 1986 or 1987—Eoin Morgan in cricket, Hugo Lloris in football, and Novak Djokovic, Andy Murray and Rafael Nadal in tennis. All of them are either World Cup or Grand Slam winners.

So is this a coincidence or is there some grand design at play?

If you draw the horoscope or the planetary positions during birth of these people, born during the same group of years, you will notice that they have certain planets in a peculiar formation. Shah Rukh Khan, Salman Khan and Aamir Khan have planet Pluto in the zodiac sign Leo at 24 degrees and the planet Neptune also at around 24 degrees. Some of the greatest actors in the world have Neptune in the charts at 24–25 degrees; for example, Marlon Brando, N.T. Rama Rao, Dilip Kumar, Dev Anand, Charlton Heston, to name a few. All the greats born in

1942 and 1946 have a planetary body I call as Planet-X around 24 degrees (in 1942) and zero degrees (in 1946). Paul McCartney, Amitabh Bachchan, Stephen Hawking, Muhammad Ali, Robert De Niro, Harrison Ford, Sylvester Stallone—all have Planet-X at 25–28 degrees. Mahatma Gandhi and Shivaji Ganesan were born with Pluto at 25 degrees. Bill Gates, Rajinikanth, Narendra Modi, Vladimir Putin, were all born with Pluto at zero degrees.

Not just that, even people who have fallen from grace or achieved huge notoriety and infamy in their lives were also born during these strategic moments. Harshad Mehta had Neptune and Pluto at zero degrees and Pablo Escobar had Pluto in zero degrees. Al Capone had Neptune at zero degrees and Osama bin Laden had it at 10 degrees. Ted Bundy had Planet-X at 10 degrees. What this clearly indicates is that the greatest in terms of any kind of work, be it good or bad, were born during certain planetary moments. They did positive things if the planets were in the right houses and negative ones if they were in the wrong houses.

And what about the rest of us?

Well, we were all born scattered around these greats, leading our moderate lives. The farther we were born from these 'peak' months, the more mediocre our lives.

Why do we need to be bothered about the zero–10–25 degrees in this book? This is for two reasons. The first one is that whenever we predict something about a person, if the person has any of the important planets in these three degrees, we know that we are talking about someone significant, in a positive or a negative way. The second reason is that whenever planets like Uranus, Neptune, Planet-X or, more importantly, Pluto move into zero, 10 or 25 degrees, they will create some events that are truly significant. The more planets in a stronger alignment, the more significant the event would be. Or the more rare the planet is (the farther it is, the rarer), the more significant the event.

One important thing to be noted is that only when a planet enters into certain zodiac signs, does the zero–10–25 rule apply; it does not apply to all zodiac signs. These houses where the planets become powerful are called as the exaltation houses. Uranus gets exalted in Aries, Gemini, Virgo and Scorpio. Neptune gets exalted in Taurus, Cancer, Libra and Sagittarius. Pluto gets exalted in Aries, Gemini, Leo, Capricorn, Aquarius and Pisces. In the other zodiac signs, these planets are not powerful and can even be weak there. The phenomenon is a bit rare and the greats are also born infrequently. The more the planets you have in these positions, the bigger the achievements. The farther the planet you have in these positions, like Saturn or Pluto instead of a Mercury or a Venus, the better.

Here are some examples of well-known people with the important planets in exaltation in zero–10–25 degrees. Just look at Shah Rukh Khan—are you surprised?

1. Albert Einstein: Planet-X-20°, Planet-Z-28°, Chiron-13°, Saturn-12°, Jupiter-5°
2. Princess Diana: Pluto-12°, Neptune-15°, Planet-Z-20°, Chiron-13°
3. Indira Gandhi: Pluto-12°, Neptune-14°, Uranus-0°, Planet-X-21°
4. Lata Mangeshkar: Pluto-26°, Planet-Z-5°, Chiron-21°
5. Mahatma Gandhi: Pluto-25°, Uranus-29°, Planet-X-2°, Jupiter-28°
6. Oprah Winfrey: Pluto-0°, Neptune-2°, Uranus-27°, Saturn-16°
7. Rajinikanth: Pluto-0°, Uranus-15°, Planet-X-2°, Chiron-0°, Jupiter-8°
8. Sachin Tendulkar: Uranus-26°, Planet-X-10°, Saturn-24°
9. Shah Rukh Khan: Pluto-24°, Neptune-25°, Planet-X-25°, Chiron-25°
10. Steve Jobs: Pluto-2°, Neptune-4°, Planet-Z-0°, Saturn-27°

The Houses of a Horoscope

This book has no intentions to make you an astrologer. The purpose is only to show that astrology works and that too along similiar lines as science—through hypothesis, evidence, observations, measurement, evaluation and extrapolation. I want to use as few astrological terms as possible to avoid any confusion. But at the same time, I cannot avoid certain technical words while explaining concepts or events. My endeavour is to make the explanations as simple as possible, though.

This book is about predicting future events using astrology. We will be talking about houses, planets and transits. The idea is not to go deeply into the technical part of the analysis. But I will share some basic information on the planetary positions.

A horoscope is a picture of the planets in their respective positions at the time of our birth, like a selfie taken at birth with the planets in the backdrop. What will unfold in our lives can be seen through the interpretation of our horoscope. There are twelve houses in a horoscope and twelve planets keep moving around these houses. Each house and planet signify a multitude of things.

We will look at the various houses and understand what they stand for. Remember that these are just a few of the indicators of those houses. Keywords are restricted to only those concepts which are discussed in this book and are not exhaustive.

A stronger planet in a house will give positive results for the areas connected with that house and vice versa. A negative planet in a house will give negative results. Similar results can also be achieved when a planet belonging to a particular house is negatively or positively placed in some other house. For example, if the ruler of the fourth house is weakly placed in the seventh house, it can give weak results of either of the house or both the houses. Also, you would note that there are some keywords or indicators which repeat themselves in different houses, like health is indicated by three houses—the sixth, the eighth and the first house. There are deeper dimensions to these but we wouldn't go there. As of now you can just take it that there are three houses that indicate health.

First house	Body, health, longevity, personality, fame, what one stands for
Second house	Wealth, money, finance, luxury
Third house	Hands, psychology, mind of a person, travels, communication
Fourth house	Home, parents, children, country of birth, local, food, land
Fifth house	Children, popularity, showbiz, media, entertainment, fashion, government
Sixth house	Health, pharma, structured work, engineering, technology, hardships
Seventh house	Marriage, relationships, arts, media, influence on people, law, politics
Eighth house	Transformation, change, sexuality, gynaecology, sports, longevity, chronic health issues, loans, bankruptcy, scandals, scams, death
Ninth house	Luck, law, spirituality, higher knowledge, foreign countries, travels
Tenth house	Career, reaching top positions, control, government
Eleventh house	Returns on the time or money invested, later part of life
Twelfth house	Legs, foreign countries, losses, working behind the scenes, hidden enemies

Take a long, hard look at this table. We will revisit this table whenever we discuss predictions. There would only be a passing reference to sixth house attributes like technology, pharma, structured work, engineering or manufacturing. We would mostly be talking about health of an individual as there would be celebrities who may face health challenges. And yes, we wouldn't be discussing any engineer, doctor or technocrat in the book.

A simple way of looking at the key indicators is that if a planet is positively placed in a particular house, one of the attributes of the house will be accentuated and the reverse will hold true if the planet is negatively placed. For example, if a sportsperson has a strong third house and if he or she is a tennis player, you know that the planet indicates the hands. Similiarly, if a politician has a strong seventh house, you know why he or she has such a huge mass appeal. At the same time, if that politician has a weaker planet in the eighth house, you know that he or she could either have a strong health issue or may be part of a scandal. These are possibilities. The more experienced you become with the patterns of the planets by seeing more horoscopes, the more logically you can arrive at what a particular planet can do.

I will mention briefly the keywords or indicators connected to each house while discussing past events and predicting the future. They will help you correlate the logic about why we talk about a certain possibility of an event occurring. Astrology is less about numbers and more about logic.

Pluto and Its Avatars

In her popular book, *Sun Signs*, Linda Goodman had talked about three personality types of Scorpios—the Eagle, the Scorpion and the Grey Lizard. I'm not sure if she had this in mind, but in my research, I observed that the ruling planet of Scorpio—Pluto—exhibits three types of manifestations while traversing within the same zodiac sign where it is exalted.

Linda says that the Eagles are the type of Scorpios who know what is the best way to take a revenge on their opponent—soar over them. They don't waste their time on planning and plotting against their opponents. The Scorpions do that. They are thin-skinned, get hurt easily and plot for revenge. The Grey Lizards are the lowest variety who keep stinging themselves and others and get caught in the dirty matters of life.

Planet Pluto, whenever it traverses any of its exaltation zodiac signs and whenever it enters zero–10–25 degrees, produces people who exhibit the characteristics of these three avatars of Scorpio. Taking a cue from Linda Goodman, I would extrapolate the characteristics of the avatars of Pluto at these exaltation points—the Eagle (zero degree), the Scorpion (25 degrees) and the Grey Lizard (10 degrees). This is the same as the three deep exaltation points of other planets. The major difference here is that the avatars of Pluto exhibit distinct characteristics of their own.

The Eagle avatar gives birth to some of the greatest innovators, pioneers, and movers and shakers in any field. They would start off as nobodys, going on to achieve extraordinary success and immortality in any field. They can be a Bill Gates, a Rajinikanth or an Oprah Winfrey. The Scorpion avatar people work hard, overcome many hurdles and finally achieve their goals. They too would go on to become great in their fields. Shah Rukh Khan, Sivaji Ganesan, Mahatma Gandhi and Dhirubhai Ambani are examples. The Grey Lizards face extraordinary struggles in life. They sometimes find themselves in excruciatingly painful situations and would come close to experiencing life's lowest. Sanjay Dutt, Michael Jackson, Anil Ambani, Lady Diana and Indira Gandhi are some examples.

While Pluto's children can be classified into these three types, the planet itself causes three kinds of events around the world while it is traversing through the exalted zodiac signs. The kind of happenings that unfold bear the characteristics of the three avatars—the Eagle, the Scorpion and the Grey Lizard. When Pluto enters into the nascent exaltation or the Eagle avatar, it brings some sort of a reset, a rebirth or a revival for a new beginning. Whenever it is in the Grey Lizard avatar there would be extraordinary problems and lows, sorrows and downright miseries in the world. When the planet reaches the Scorpion avatar, it brings out the highest glories after all the lows and builds it up to a crescendo.

This becomes even more dramatic when Pluto is in debilitation in any zodiac sign. Pluto brings in new hitches, depths of despair and huge collapses during the three avatars, especially when in reaches the Grey Lizard patch while in debilitation. The entire journey of Pluto through the different zodiac signs in exaltation and debilitation creates numerous fascinating events which define decades and sometimes even centuries.

How Pluto Changes the World Order

Ever wondered why one day you get very engrossed in data even though you are actually not a data-oriented person, and on another day you feel extremely touchy and emotional while you are not so normally? This happens because the Moon changes zodiac signs every two-and-half days and the zodiac sign in which the Moon was traversing influences our moods on those days. The Moon is the closest to earth and its impact is only on the emotions. The other bodies and planets which are closer to us, like the Sun, Mercury, Venus and Mars, also impact our daily lives in a subtle way.

Planets like Jupiter, Saturn and those beyond not only influence us but also everything around us—including business, trade, markets, sports and every event that happens across the world. The study of the influence of planets on everyday life is called 'mundane astrology'. Mundane astrology can be further classified into areas like finance astrology, sports astrology or political astrology.

Planets are generally in four states—own house, fall house, exaltation house and debilitation house. Own house means the zodiac sign with which the particular planet is associated. The particular zodiac sign resonates with the traits of the planet and the planet exhibits positive results while traversing through that zodiac sign. Librans are artistic, creative, empathic and love the concept called 'love'. Libra is assigned as the 'own' house of Venus.

A planet gets exalted in another zodiac sign wherein some of the traits of the planet get even more amplified. Venus gets exalted in Pisces. Pisceans are artistic, creative and surrender themselves in love. They are the epitome of love, peace and harmony. Hence Venus gets exalted in Pisces. Venus is in fall in the zodiac sign Aries. On the wheel of the zodiac, Aries is exactly opposite to Libra. Venus loses its power there in its opposite house and is called as 'in fall'. Arians are more self-motivated and aren't exactly known to be artistic, empathic or soft-mannered. They are the exact anti-thesis of what Libra stands for. Virgo falls exactly opposite Pisces, the zodiac sign where Venus gets exalted. Virgos are very matter-of-fact in love, aren't very romantic, are loners and are generally more pragmatic, showing clearly the traits which are contrary to the natural traits of Venus. This is because Venus is debilitated in Virgo.

This is an example of just Venus. Similarly, every planet has its own house, fall house, and several exaltation and debilitation houses. Planets which are farther, starting from Jupiter, have multiple exaltation and debilitation points.

Planets like Chiron, Jupiter, Saturn, Planet-Y and Planet-Z influence major events in the world. Chiron rules real estate, land and property. If Chiron is in a negative transit, which means if it is in fall or in debilitation, then the real estate industry doesn't do well, the property prices plunge or there is a decrease in demand. The transit of Jupiter, the largest planet, into most zodiac signs indicate growth and increase in opportunity while Saturn indicates contraction and truncation of growth.

When Planet-X is in Taurus, its own zodiac sign, it signals a free flow of capital and currency. When it is in deepest exaltation in Aquarius, it fuels the economy. When Planet-X gets into debilitation in the zodiac sign of Leo or is in fall in Scorpio, the world goes through complications in currency movement, businesses become dull and there is a general lull in the market. The entire economic cycle can be connected to the movement of Planet-X. The biggest highs and the biggest meltdowns have coincided with the best and the worst transits of Planet-X.

The movement of Planet-Y influences the production capacity, labour and also indicates the general state of the health industry. Planet-Z is connected with everything which is showy—the media, entertainment and the showbiz world.

The largest influencers from the solar system are Uranus, Neptune and Pluto. Uranus signifies the sudden changes that happen which change the dynamics of the situation. Neptune is a very interesting planet which can either bring in some positive energy or create some confusion.

All of these bodies exert their own power and bring in either positive or negative manifestations. But the biggest influencer of them is Pluto. The biggest changes or biggest transformations are caused by Pluto. All work that the other planets do are subset of the work of Pluto. Pluto produces generational changes; all the other planets do their work, within the range of the work of Pluto. Pluto is clearly the boss. A boss occupies the corner seat in the office and Pluto definitely is in the farthest corner.

In the subsequent chapters, we will see what major transformations Pluto brings about. Pluto creates an extraordinary journey in a particular zodiac sign and all the other planets play second, third or fourth fiddle to the master. The rest of the planets do their job and the minor variations from them actually prove that Pluto has been the master of fate and destiny over the time.

Pluto can influence the mindset of a generation and make them reckless in spending their money. It can make an entire generation to rock-and-roll or go spiritual or fight against oppression. While this merry-making is going on, due to Uranus getting into debilitation, there could be a fall in the markets and as Uranus is involved, it could be sudden. Adding to the woes, Neptune may go into debilitation too and there would be sudden confusion and chaos everywhere. This would go on till Pluto gets into a stronger position once again after a few months or years. Thus Pluto is the conductor of the orchestra and the entire setting and all the other planets play along.

We will see what Pluto has done in the past few centuries when it has moved across zodiac signs. The various keywords of a particular zodiac sign indicate the probable areas in which Pluto would exert its influence. Depending upon the 'state' of Pluto, the events could be positive or negative. The results would be positive if the planet is in an exalted state or in its own house, and negative if it is in debilitation.

If we want to predict what Pluto can do in the future, we need to understand what it has done in the past. The past, most of the time, holds the key to knowing the future.

Pluto in Scorpio (1742–1757): Era of New Establishments

Pluto in its own house
The Seven Years' War (1756–1763); American colonies becoming self-sufficent (1750s); Battle of Plassey (1757); East India Company achieves trade monopoly

What are the key qualities of Scorpio? A strong desire to dominate and control, the need to achieve power and keep growing and transforming. You will see all these qualities on display when Pluto enters Scorpio.

The famed story of America had its beginnings with the de facto first prime minister of Britain, Sir Robert Walpole's control or the absence of it on the colonies. Before Pluto entered Scorpio in 1742, it was in Libra in the 1730s. One of the important things that Libra rules is the law and Pluto gets debilitated in Libra. This means there is a laxity in following rules and regulations. In an effort to increase tax income, Walpole was lax in the enforcement of trade laws and reduced regulations, stating that if no restrictions were placed on the colonies, they would flourish. This resulted in the neglect of the colonies.[9]

When Pluto transited into Scorpio, the colonies of America became stronger and self-sufficient. Pluto in Scorpio made the residents of America stronger and prepared for the battles ahead.

At around the same time, in India, the East India Company, which was started as a trade organisation, went on to acquire a complete monopoly of trade. For India and America, these were precursors of some huge events to follow. Pluto had done a reset that went on to redefine the fate of the two countries in the centuries to come.

Pluto in Sagittarius (1758–1772): Era of Lawlessness and Insurgency

Pluto in debilitation
Eagle patch (1758–1759): Native Americans suppressed; Rule of the British Raj in India
Grey Lizard patch (1761–1763): Royal Proclamation of 1763
Scorpion patch (1769–1771): Boston Massacre; Gaspee Affair; Great Bengal Famine

....

Sagittarians wants to cut loose, break free and soar high. At the same time, Sagittarius also rules the law, being the natural ninth zodiac sign. When Pluto enters into Sagittarius, exactly the opposite thing happens; lawlessness prevails, as Pluto is debilitated here.

During 1758–1772, the resident Americans were suppressed, controlled and dominated by the European colonial powers. The seeds of the American Revolution were sown during the debilitated phase of Pluto in Sagittarius. The word 'revolution' may seem positive but every revolution leaves a lot of blood and sorrow in its trail.

---

[9]   James Henretta, 'Salutary Neglect', *Encyclopedia Virginia*, 7 December 2020, https://www.encyclopediavirginia.org/salutary_neglect#start_entry.

In India, the last Nawab of Bengal, Siraj-ud-Daulah, was tricked by Robert Clive in the Battle of Plassey.[10] The British official bribed Mir Jafar, the military general of the Nawab, and defeated him. The devastation from the war and exploitative tax policies after 1765, aimed at revenue maximisation by the rapacious British East India Company, crippled the economic resources of the rural population and resulted in the death of about 10 million Indians.[11]

Pluto in Sagittarius was favouring Robert Clive to light a spark which would eventually engulf the entire Indian subcontinent. And it all began with a circumvention or wrong enforcement of the law, the natural domain of Sagittarius.

Pluto in Capricorn (1773–1792): Era of Establishing the Empire

Pluto in exaltation
Eagle patch (1773–1776): American War of Independence; United States of America established
Grey Lizard patch (1778–1780): Southern theatre of the American Revolutionary War; Carlisle Peace Commission
Scorpion patch (1788–1792): French Revolution; Haitian Revolution; Australian Frontier wars

Capricorn is about career. It is about taking control of your territory and of what you feel is rightfully yours. Capricorns will do anything for the family. It is about taking care of your own and your loved one's needs.

The American War of Independence against the British happened during the transit of Pluto into Capricorn. Many national leaders met in Philadelphia in 1787 to establish a new constitution. The new constitution was ratified in 1788, and a new federal government was formed in 1789.

---

10   Hugh Chisholm, ed., 'Clive, Robert Clive, Baron', *Encyclopaedia Britannica*, 11th ed. (Cambridge University Press, 2011), pp. 532–36.
11   William Dalrymple, 'The East India Company: The Original Corporate Raiders', *The Guardian*, 4 March 2015.

This was also a period when the ancient regime was abolished in favour of constitutional monarchy in France. The French Revolution ended feudalism in France, emancipated individuals, and created nominal equality of citizens. This was not just about France. It was a globally significant event, as it exported principles such as liberalism, political radicalism, nationalism and secularism.[12]

In India, the British East India Company established a capital in Calcutta in 1773. It was given the right to collect revenue in Bengal and Bihar. It also appointed Warren Hastings as its first governor general and became directly involved in governance.[13]

Pluto in Aquarius (1792–1816): Era of Egalitarianism and Fight for Independence

Pluto in exaltation
Eagle patch (1792–93): French Revolutionary wars and abolition of monarchy
Grey Lizard patch (1796–1801): Napoleonic wars; Battle of Seringapatam
Scorpion patch (1810–16): Peace Congress of Vienna; Independence of Columbia and Venezuelan; Mexican Wars of Independence

Aquarius is all about equality, brotherhood and rising above social-class divide. When Pluto traversed through Aquarius, these virtues shone through. The UK abolished slave trade in 1807. American President Thomas Jefferson was an egalitarian. He believed in the principle that all people are equal and deserve equal rights and opportunities with priority for the 'yeoman farmer', 'planters', and the 'plain folk'.[14]

[12] James Livesey, *Making Democracy in the French Revolution* (Harvard University Press, 2001).

[13] Barbara Daly Metcalf and Thomas R. Metcalf, *A Concise History of Modern India* (Cambridge University Press, 2006).

[14] Gordon S Wood, *The American Revolution: A History (Modern Library Chronicles)*, (Hansebooks, 2003) p. 100.

The Sikh Empire established by Maharaja Ranjit Singh based in the Punjab was secular. The Sikh Empire was distinctive in that it allowed men from other religions also to rise to commanding positions of authority.[15]

Aquarius is also connected to science, inventions and discoveries. In the UK, Edward Jenner created the first vaccine—for smallpox. The birth of the rail transport started with Richard Trevithick's steam locomotive in 1804. In 1812, the first commercial rail started running in the UK.

Aquarius is also about fierce spirit of independence. The wars fought by Napoleon had profound consequences for global history, including the spread of nationalism and liberalism, the appearance of independence movements in Latin America and subsequent collapse of the Spanish and Portuguese empires and the fundamental reorganisation of German and Italian territories into larger states.

Pluto in Pisces (1816–1844): Era of Good Feelings

Pluto in exaltation
Eagle patch (1816-1817): Society for promotion of permanent and universal peace; Argentina, Uruguay and Bolivia declare independence
Grey Lizard patch (1823-1828): Mexico becomes a republic
Scorpion patch (1838-1844): Ether as anaesthetic (US); Pilsner is brewed; Thames Tunnel opened; Camera patented

Pisces is all about empathy, peace, happiness, live and let live. Pisceans are also very spiritual. This part of the American history is called the 'Era of Good Feelings'. It saw a trend towards loyalty to the nation recognising government's role in nation building that envisioned 'a permanent federal role in the crucial arena of national development and national prosperity'.[16] This was also a

---

[15] Kartar Singh Duggal, *Maharaja Ranjit Singh: The Last to Lay Arms* (Abhinav Publications, 2001), pp. 125–126.

[16] Andrew Berstein and Nancy Issenberg, *Madison and Jefferson* (Random House, 2010).

period of spiritual evolution and a belief in higher manifestations. It was believed that American settlers were destined to expand across North America.[17]

Maharaj Ranjit Singh overlaid the sanctum of Harmandir Sahib in Amritsar with gold in the year 1830, emphasising the spiritual aspect of Pluto in Pisces. This led to its name 'Golden Temple'.[18]

Pisceans hate any kind of pain, especially the physical kind. Crawford Long used ether as an anaesthetic in surgery for the first time in Georgia in 1842. Samuel Morse discovered Morse code and introduced telegraphy, probably helping Pisceans SOS someone when in distress.

When Pluto entered the peace-loving Pisces, the wars ended and resulted in the independence of several countries in South America—Argentina in 1816, Chile in 1818, Ecuador in 1819, Panama, Peru in 1821, Ecuador in 1822 and Uruguay in 1825.

Pluto in Aries (1844–1876): Era of Rebellion and Reconstruction

Pluto in exaltation
Eagle patch (1844–45): Bahá'í faith established; YMCA, The Great Famine
Grey Lizard patch (1853–58): Crimean War, Indian Rebellion of 1857; The panic of 1857
Scorpion patch (1869–1876): Black Friday; Suez Canal opened; Alexander Graham Bell invents telephone

Aries is all about aggression, passion, rebellion and taking on a street fight. When Pluto traverses through Aries, it invokes passion in people. As Aries is the most ruthless amongst all zodiac signs, the resultant manifestations are also bloody and gory.

[17] 'Manifest Destiny', *US History*, https://www.ushistory.org/us/29.asp.
[18] Jean Marie Lafont, *Maharaja Ranjit Singh: Lord of the Five Rivers* (Oxford University Press, 2002), pp. 95–96.

The American Civil War against slavery was one of the bloodiest wars that ever took place. It was the greatest moral, constitutional and political crisis ever in America.[19]

The first Indian War of Independence, also called as Indian Rebellion of 1857, was also fought during this period. Violence, which sometimes betrayed exceptional cruelty, was inflicted on both sides.[20]

Karl Marx and Friedrich Engels published *The Communist Manifesto, Which Explains History in Terms of Class Struggle and Proposes That Workers Unite and Overthrow Capitalism* in 1848 in the UK.

In 1848, *The Declaration of Sentiments*, written by Elizabeth Cady Stanton and signed at the Women's Rights Convention in Seneca Falls, New York, US, called for giving women the right to vote.

Violence, anger, resentment, rebellion and fight for rights rules when Pluto traverses Aries.

Pluto in Taurus (1876–1901): Era of Huge Class Divide and Systematic Soft Power

Pluto in fall throughout (1876–1901)

Queen Victoria proclaimed Empress of India; Northern-Chinese famine of 1876–1879; Panic of 1893, Great railroad strike; Bituminous coal-miners' strike; Russo-Turkish war; War of the Pacific; Gilded age.

Taurus rules money, wealth and prosperity. Pluto is in a 'fall' position when it traverses through Taurus and everything connected to Taurus would be on a downward trend. While a handful of people held all the reigns and finance, common people fell at the other end of the spectrum indicating the huge class-divide of this period. The rapid expansion of

---

[19] John Huddleston, *Killing Ground: The Civil War and the Changing American Landscape* (Johns Hopkins University Press, 2002).

[20] P.J. Marshall, '1783–1870: An Expanding Empire', in P.J. Marshall (ed.), *The Cambridge Illustrated History of the British Empire* (Cambridge University Press, 2001), p. 50.

industrialisation led to a real wage growth of 60 per cent, from the 1870s to about 1900. Conversely, this was also an era of abject poverty and inequality, as millions of immigrants—many from impoverished regions—poured into the United States, and the high concentration of wealth became more visible and contentious.[21]

By the end of the nineteenth century, India was Britain's biggest cash-cow, the world's biggest purchaser of British exports and the source of highly paid employment for British civil servants—all at India's own expense.[22]

The Berlin Conference of 1884, which regulated European colonisation and trade in Africa, is the starting point of the 'Scramble for Africa'. Partitioning Africa was effected largely without Europeans going to war.[23] Taureans love their peace—acquire wealth and territories but without actually fighting for it!

Pluto in Gemini (1901–1929): Era of Miscommunication, Communication, Fun and Frolic

Pluto in exaltation
Eagle patch (1901–1902): Antarctic Expedition; first powered flight; first movie theatre
Grey Lizard patch (1914–1920): World War I, Einstein shows E = mc2, ; Russian Revolution; Spanish Flu; First Radio news, First passenger airline, First transatlantic flight
Scorpion patch (1926–1929): First colour TV; First Academy Awards; First transpacific flight

Gemini embodies intelligence, communication, movement and is a fun zodiac sign. When Pluto traversed Gemini during the Eagle and Scorpion patches, all the positive aspects of Gemini

21   Joseph Stiglitz, *The Price of Inequality: How Today's Divided Society Endangers Our Future* (W.W. Norton & Company, 2013), p. xxxiv.

22   https://www.bbc.com/news/world-asia-india-33618621

23   R. Robinson, J. Gallagher and A. Denny, *Africa and the Victorians* (1965), p. 175.

shone through while the worst of Gemini came out during the Grey Lizard patch.

'A confused group of politicians who are overtaken by events. And, as a consequence of that, they are trapped occasionally into taking decisions which gently, gradually lead to the process of the outbreak of war.'[24] Gerhard Hirschfeld, professor of history at the University of Stuttgart, shows that it was a series of miscommunications that led to the war and its escalation.

Immediately after the ill-effects of Pluto in the Grey Lizard leading to World War I, what followed was a transformed fun and frolic Geminian era. This period saw large-scale development of automobiles, telephones, movies, radio and electrical appliances. Aviation soon became a big business. The spirit of the Roaring Twenties, the popularity of jazz and dancing in opposition to the mood of WWI also led this period to be referred to as the Jazz Age.[25]

Pluto in Cancer (1929–1949): An Era That Destabilised Roots

Pluto in debilitation
Eagle patch (1929–1931): The Great Depression; Kazakh, Soviet and Ukraine famine
Grey Lizard patch (1939–1943): World War II; The holocaust
Scorpion patch (1946–1949): Countries carved out; Partition; Decolonisation, Apartheid

....

The zodiac sign of Cancer stands for food, home, children, family, land, motherland. When Pluto traverses through Cancer, it creates the worst situation for all the indicators of the fourth house. The Great Depression of the 1930s uprooted families and rendered many people homeless and unemployed.

---

[24] Dragan Stavljanin, 'World War I Anniversary: Five Historians, Two Questions', *Radio Free Europe/Radio Liberty*, 28 July 2014, https://www.rferl.org/a/wwi-key-questions-war-anniversary-historians/25472768.html.

[25] Jody Blake, *Le Tumulte Noir: Modernist Art and Popular Entertainment in Jazz-Age Paris, 1900–1930* (Pennsylvania State University Press, 1999).

Adolf Hitler came with his own prejudices against an ethno-religious group—the Jews—and exterminated six million of them, including one million children. World War II started in 1939. Atomic bombs were dropped on Hiroshima and Nagasaki. Two lakh people died and many were rendered homeless, and then there was the long-term effect of children being born with genetic disorders.[26]

Mahatma Gandhi initiated the 'Quit India' movement against the British in 1942, the Cancerian Pluto asking the captors to leave its home. The only positive aspect of Pluto in Cancer was that countries were able to drive out their captors from their homelands. India (1947), Pakistan (1947), Taiwan (1948), North Vietnam (1945), Northern China (1945), Korea (1945), Indonesia (1945), Burma (1948), Ceylon (1948) and Israel (1948) were some of the beneficiaries.

Post the World War, countries carved out and also partitioned. Partition of a country is like cutting down your own home into pieces. As Pluto was in debilitation, the de-colonisation and partition happened in the cruellest of ways.

Pluto in Leo (1949–1969): Era of Gaining Your Pride and Working Towards Glory

Pluto in exaltation

Eagle patch (1949–1951): India becomes a democracy; People's Republic of China established; UNIVAC-1—first digital computer for business applications—released

Grey Lizard patch (1958–1961): The Great Chinese Famine; Tibetan uprising; Congo crisis; Construction of Berlin wall; First contraceptive pills; NASA established

Scorpion patch (1964–1969): Indo-Pak war; Intelsat I—first communications satellite—launched; BASIC programming language launched; Man landed on moon; ISRO established

---

[26] 'Birth defects among the children of atomic-bomb survivors (1948–1954)', *Radiation Effects Research Foundation*, https://www.rerf.or.jp/en/programs/roadmap_e/health_effects-en/geneefx-en/birthdef/, accessed 31 Dec 2020.

For a Leo the canvas is always large; they aim for bigger glory and love being leaders. Leos have an innate understanding of technology and how it works. And yes, Leos have their pride.

Martin Luther King Jr. was the main architect on the civil rights movement, which eventually led to the Civil Rights Act of 1964. In 1952, Nelson Mandela[27] started defiance campaigns against Apartheid, which became a larger movement in South Africa. In her 1963 book *The Feminine Mystique*, Betty Friedan questioned the women's magazines, women's education system and advertisers for creating the widespread image of women contented with just being housewives and mothers and demanded to be treated with as much respect as the men.

In the US, new music genres such as rock-and-roll as well as fashion styles and subcultures like 'greaser' were formed, men who drove motorcycles, sported ducktail haircuts and displayed a general disregard for the law and authority.[28]

The Leo's penchant for achieving huge milestones in terms of technology saw the Russians launch Sputnik, the first artificial satellite of earth, in the 1950s and the Americans put a human on the moon in 1969.

Pluto in Virgo (1970–1980): Era of Polishing Self and Awareness of Surroundings

Pluto in neutral state
Eagle patch (1970–1971): Earth day; Treaty on the Non-Proliferation of Nuclear Weapons
Grey Lizard patch (1972–1974): Indo-Pak war and liberation of Bangladesh; Watergate scandal
Scorpion patch (1978–1980): Test-tube baby; One-child policy in China; Iranian Revolution

---

[27] Mary Benson, *Nelson Mandela* (Penguin Books, 1986).
[28] William H. Chafe, *The Unfinished Journey: America Since World War II* (Oxford University Press, 2011).

In Virgo, Pluto is neither exalted, nor debilitated, probably indicating the nature of Virgos—being neutral. They are so much into themselves and their work—and doing it meticulously. 'The "Me Decade" (1970s) fostered atomised individualism. The new alchemical dream is: changing one's personality—remaking, remodelling, elevating, and polishing one's very self.'[29]

The Cambodian Genocide (1975–1979) resulted in two million deaths. The Khmer Rouge used an inhumane forced labour regime, starvation and state terror to keep the population in line. One Khmer Rouge leader said the killings were meant for the 'purification of the populace'.[30] The sixth house, with which the zodiac sign of Virgo resonates, is connected with hard labour and starvation. Ironically, the word 'purity' too is associated with Virgo.

Virgos care for their environment. On 22 April 1970, 20 million Americans took to the streets against the deterioration of the environment. Greenpeace, an NGO that works on climate change, deforestation, genetic engineering and anti-nuclear issues, was founded in 1971.[31] Nuclear non-proliferation treaty came into effect in 1970.

Pluto in Libra (1980–1989): Era of Indulgence, Carelessness and Lawlessness

Pluto in debilitation
Eagle patch (1980–1981): Riots in England, St. Paul, New Mexico and Brixton; Coups in Turkey; Suriname and Liberia; Internal conflicts in Sri Lanka and Peru; Iran-Iraq war
Grey Lizard patch (1984–1986): Chernobyl disaster; Bhopal gas tragedy; Challenger disaster; Operation Blue Star; Assassination of Indira Gandhi; anti-Sikh riots

---

29   Carol McNamara, 'The Pursuit of Happiness, American Style: Tom Wolfe's Study of Status and Freedom', *Perspectives on Political Science*, vol. 34, issue 1, 2005.

30   Hurst Hannum, 'International Law and Cambodian Genocide: The Sounds of Silence', *Human Rights Quarterly*, vol. 11, no. 1 February 1989, pp. 82–138, https://doi.org/10.2307/761936.

31   Greenpeace, https://www.greenpeace.org/usa/about/

Scorpion patch (1988–1989); HIV emerges as a pandemic; Singing Revolution; 8888 uprising; Al-Qaeda formed; Velvet Revolution

Libra stands for all the nicer things in life, like love and relationships. It is very unfortunate that Pluto gets debilitated here. The ugliness that comes when love is in its most careless form came to the fore in the form of HIV emerging as a pandemic.

The decade of the eighties was full of episodes of demonstrations, strikes, sieges, assassinations, air attacks, civil wars, coups—generally incidents which could cause the law and order situation to go out of control. Clearly, 'law', an area connected to Libra, is at its lowest when Pluto traverses Libra. The US President Ronald Reagan launched an attack on the drug cartels to put an end to the menace of crack (cocaine) epidemic.[32]

The Chernobyl disaster and the Bhopal gas tragedy happened due to human errors. Moments of madness when people don't comply to the rules and regulations have resulted in disasters.

Libra also rules peace. General Secretary of the Communist Party of Soviet Union Mikhail Gorbachev and US president Ronald Reagan met multiple times in numerous summits in the 1980s. These meetings finally led to the end of the Cold War between the two nations in 1991, after more than four decades.

Pluto in Scorpio (1989–2005): Era of Opening Up of Opportunities

Pluto in own house throughout
Collapse of Soviet Union; Fall of Berlin Wall; Reunification of Germany; Formation of the European Union and introduction of the euro; Harshad Mehta scam in India, Economic liberalisation in India, End of apartheid in South Africa

---

[32] Interview with Eric E. Sterling, *Frontline*, https://www.pbs.org/wgbh/pages/frontline/shows/snitch/procon/sterling.html

Tim Berners-Lee invented the world wide web in 1989–1990 which, together with internet, changed the way the world operates. The biggest invention of the millennium that will transform the world completely couldn't have happened at any other time than when Pluto entered into its own house after almost 250 years.

The Soviet Union collapsed and this could be the best thing that could have happened to Russia. It was leaner and could be more efficient. Nelson Mandela led South Africans to break the shackles of apartheid. Many of those born in India in the 1970s and 1980s owe their careers to the liberalisation of economy in India, starting in 1991.

The Berlin Wall fell to the happy tears of many. East and West Germany were reunited. The European countries came together and formed the European Union and later introduced euro as their common currency.

The Harshad Mehta scam led to the biggest clean-up of the financial system in India. Securities and Exchange Board of India (SEBI) was established as the watchdog of the industry.

Pluto's entry into its own house coincided with the rise in terrorism. Pluto rules the underworld and everything that is menacing and polarising. The twin towers attack on 11 September 2001 was an indicator that organised terrorism was going to be a part of modern life.

Pluto in Sagittarius (2006–2019): Era of Recklessness, Uprising and Coming Out

Pluto in debilitation
Eagle patch (2006–2007): Bomb blasts in Mumbai and Baghdad; Great Recession
Grey Lizard patch (2009–2011): Arab spring, Horizon oil spill, Euozone crisis
Scorpion patch (2016–2019): #MeToo movement; Panama Papers leak; Hong Kong protests

Sagittarians are highly risk-taking and wouldn't really bother if they have flouted a couple of rules while aiming recklessly for the stars. The subprime crisis of 2008 was triggered by excessive risk-taking by financial institutions in the form of excessive credit.[33]

Sagittarians stand up and fight against any injustice. Mohamed Bouazizi, a fruit-seller in Tunisia, immolated himself to protest against harassment of municipal officers. This led to the Arab Spring, and the overthrowing of governments of Tunisia, Libra and Egypt. [34]

Spirituality and law are ruled by Sagittarius. Asaram Bapu, Swami Nityananda and Gurmeet Ram Rahim Singh were exposed due to financial or sexual malpractices.[35] Many mighty men with a sexual predatory past fell in the #MeToo movement.[36] Nirav Modi, Vijay Mallya and Subrato Roy were those flamboyant (Sagittarius again) corporate honchos who took the rules of the land for granted and paid the price.[37]

---

[33] Mark Williams, *Uncontrolled Risk: Lessons of Lehman Brothers and How Systemic Risk Can Still Bring Down the World Financial System* (McGraw-Hill Education, 2010), pp. 213.

[34] 'Arab Spring', *History*, 10 January 2018, https://www.history.com/topics/middle-east/arab-spring

[35] Aviral Virk, 'The Full List of Fake Indian Babas Who've Been Blacklisted', *The Quint*, 13 September 2017, https://www.thequint.com/news/india/fake-indian-babas-godmen-blacklisted.

[36] Stephanie Zacharek, Eliana Dockterman and Haley Sweetland Edwards, 'Person of the Year 2017: *The Silence Breakers*', *Time*, https://time.com/time-person-of-the-year-2017-silence-breakers/.

[37] Sidharth Bhatia, 'India's Big Bad Billionaires Are United in Their Arrogance, Entitlement and Disdain for Laws', *The Wire*, 12 October 2020, https://thewire.in/film/bad-boy-billionaires-netflix-nirav-modi-vijay-mallya-subrata-roy-arrogance-entitlement-disdain-laws.

Terminology
You Should Know

These are some terms you will see frequently in the book, and you need to know them. Their simplest meanings are explained here without going too much into specifics.

New Moon: When the Sun and the Moon are in the same zodiac sign, and the Moon is ahead of the Sun. E.g., when the Sun and the Moon are in Cancer, the Sun is at 11 degrees and the Moon is at 14 degrees. The closer the Moon is to the Sun, the more auspicious it is.

Full Moon: When the Sun and the Moon are in exactly opposite zodiac signs. E.g., the Sun is in Aries at 17 degrees, and the Moon is in Libra at 15 degrees. The complete full moon is when the degree of the Sun and the Moon are exactly the same. So, when both the Sun and the Moon both are at 17 degrees, it is an extremely powerful and auspicious time. In this example, as the Moon moves towards 17 degrees, it slowly becomes fuller and waxes. Once it crosses the full Moon degree, it starts waning and then it isn't favourable.

Amavasya (no moon): When the Sun and the Moon are in the same zodiac sign, but the Moon is behind the Sun. E.g., the Sun is in Virgo at 17 degrees and the Moon is in Virgo at 14 degrees. In this example, when Sun is at 14 degrees, the Moon will be mildly weaker when it enters Virgo at zero degrees. It will enter deep amavasya or a complete no-moon period when it is precisely at 17 degrees and, just after it crosses 17 degrees, it will become a new moon. The amavasya period is generally considered inauspicious. Amavasya needn't necessarily happen only during night. It can happen even during the day.

Planet in 'dignity': A planet is considered to be in 'dignity' when it is in its own house or the house of exaltation, or is full (in case of moon), or new (in case of moon). Generally, it is a positive placement.

Manglik: A commonly used, but a very highly misunderstood term. Manglik is the position of Mars in any of these houses in an individual's birth chart: first, fourth, seventh, eighth or twelfth. In these positions, Mars can pose challenges to an individual in the area of relationships. 1/4/7/12/8 is the increasing order of the severity of the problems according to the houses. Most importantly, we need to consider them with the planets in, and the rulers of, the seventh house (marriage) to get the complete picture.

Karmic quota: We begin with the premise that all human beings come to the world with a certain quota of success/happiness and failure/misery, based on their past lives (karma), that play out during their lifetime. No one will face more or less than what is due to them. Karmic quota is the process of calculating the impact of a planet upon a person—whether positive or negative—and the number of years the impact will last. The calculations are based on the strength of the planet in the birth chart, and its movement into different zodiac signs over the years. It involves knowing the exact ways in which the effects of the planet have already manifested themselves, and calculating its remaining impact for the future.

Predictions

Prediction #1
Pluto in Capricorn (2019-2039): Era of 'Going Back Home'
Pluto in exaltation throughout

During the entire first half of 2019, I wondered what Pluto would do when it came back to Capricorn in the last quarter of the year. If we look at the last twelve eras of Pluto in the various zodiac signs, we notice that it is difficult to predict exactly which area of a particular zodiac sign Pluto will impact. It is only after the event has happened that we realise that it was how everything was supposed to be. In other words, we anticipate the final outcome, but we don't know what events would trigger that ultimate manifestation. But we can maintain a list of aspects the planet can impact, and keep our eyes on certain possibilities.

A Capricorn wants to rule the world but, at the same time, wants to spend quality time with the family. Capricorns would work hard, and scheme and plot and plan to win over the enemy to reach the top but, at the same time, would revere tradition and follow the old schools of thought. Now which one of these things Pluto would impact at the end of 2019 was anybody's guess. But, in the nascent exaltation in the Eagle patch, something dramatic was supposed to happen, which would ultimately lead to the final manifestation. It did happen—and how!

By March 2020, it was very clear that Covid-19 was proof that Pluto had already entered Capricorn, and was in the Eagle patch. And when Covid-19 spread and became a pandemic, the theme of the era dawned upon me. I shared my views in a

YouTube video about the changes we were about to witness.[38] I spoke about how the workplaces across the world would be transformed—and we can see it happening already.

Pluto will stay in Capricorn from 2020–2038 and its transformation acts, connected with Capricorn, will happen over a period of the next two decades, that is, the 2020s and the 2030s. Regardless of the current devastation, eventually, it will turn out to be a positive reset, as Pluto gets exalted here.

So, what is this era all about?

The Capricorn values are centred on family, career, possessions and ambition. The last time Pluto was in Capricorn, in the eighteenth century, the focus was more on claiming your territory, and taking the reins in your hands. That was the beginning of the great American story, and the establishment of the British empire in India. But, this time, it's all about your family. Well, that is what it seems like—as of now.

Over the last three eras, since the time Pluto was in Libra, there has been recklessness in the way we have been doing everything. We were flouting rules. We spent most of our time outside our homes. Pluto's entry in Capricorn has come to remind us of the values we have forgotten. The biggest reset Covid-19 has caused is that it has brought us back to our families. We have come closer to one another, and learnt to share the responsibilities. We have rediscovered the 'essentials' in life.

Capricorn is the natural ruler of the tenth house, and the tenth house indicates a formal (corporate) career. And what a dramatic change Pluto has created in terms of the workplace! In 2017, as a human resources (HR) professional, I was responsible for skill development at a multinational corporation (MNC). During a discussion with my boss, the head of HR, I mentioned that in Europe some companies

---

[38] Greenstone Lobo, 'How Long Will Corona Virus Impact?', *YouTube*, 21 March 2020, https://www.youtube.com/watch?v=4zAHJBbVQZ0&t=719s.

had implemented a four-and-a-half-day work-week and it had given them good results. My boss said it was impractical and that such a fancy idea would never work in India. People would only abuse this privilege, dodge their responsibilities, and productivity would plummet. Being aware of Pluto's entry in Capricorn in 2020, I told him that this would actually become inevitable in the 2020s, and it would actually work wonders. People would have greater work-life balance, they would be more productive, and the formal work structure would change. Well, he wasn't in a mood to listen.

Looking back, I can pat my back that I was correct. What a reset it has been! The corporates have realised that you really don't need a physical, expensive structure for an office. Work can be done from remote locations, without quality being compromised. There is decentralisation of work. People have travelled back to their hometowns and work from there.

Now most people spend a reasonable amount of time in their homes. This has become a norm, and most corporates are not going back to the old structure—besides other benefits, they have realised it saves them huge costs. People can work from the comfort of their homes and still deliver—a dream come true for every Capricorn! The next two decades will be about further exploring and extending this idea. Innovative workspaces and huge changes in the way we work can be expected. And people who took a break from work because of responsibilities towards their family will now have opportunities opening up for them like never before.

At the same time, we should remember Capricorn's urge to grow and take control. The next two decades are also going to be about one-upmanship. In some part of the world there will be a country which will try to expand its territory. Watch all the top countries of the world. The fight to be at the top will make them behave irrationally. Skirmishes at the border, territorial wars and mini wars cannot be ruled out.

There will be a group of people in some countries who will want power and position. And, if that can come only from a split in territories, then that may happen too. Therefore some countries where there is already some infighting, which started in the Sagittarius patch, will undergo huge transformations. Expect some new countries to be carved out of the existing ones, and bigger ones breaking into smaller fragments.

Another World War? I really don't think so. The top three planets—Uranus, Neptune and Pluto—have to enter seriously problematic positions, and the transit has to be in a debilitated zodiac sign, for that kind of a calamity to happen. Mercifully, it isn't so at the moment. We can breathe easy on that count.

Prediction #2
Neptune Enters Pisces in Zero Degrees (2021–2022)

When you are writing a book on predictions, there is always a possibility that one of those may come true even before the book is published.

Neptune was slated to enter its own zodiac sign, Pisces, in March 2021 after 165 years. It will hover around zero to one degree in Pisces till the mid of 2022 and stay put there for another fourteen years. During this long stay, it will cause some very positive and also some very challenging events. But at the same time, the planet will signal some kind of a warning through some major tragedy or there could be a series of small but impactful events signalling Neptune's entry into Pisces—and during its stay in zero to one degrees—during 2021–2022.

I had been expecting Neptune to announce its arrival through some incident involving water. I resisted the temptation to put up a YouTube video for some time, as I wanted to keep these predictions exclusively for this book. A week after I finished writing the outline of this prediction, however, one of the worst glacier bursts occurred in the Uttarakhand district of the Himalayas, with a few hundred people losing their lives.[39] It was a clear indication that Neptune had already arrived on the horizon. So, I put up a YouTube video[40] in February 2021, which outlines the various keywords connected to Neptune that we need to keep a watch on—water, make believe, illusion, spirituality, ether, gas, tragedy and magic.

Since February 2021 till the time this article was revised and updated, I was amazed to see so many events that clearly indicated Neptune's mischiefs. Suez Canal obstruction, once-in-100 years floods in Australia, the iceberg splitting from Antartica, Tauktae cyclone, Iceland's volcanic eruptions, Taiwan's drought, Indonesian submarine went missing, flooding in Morocco—it is shocking to see water-related events gushing in just three to four months. The worry is that this isn't over yet.

We still have more than a year to go till Neptune would be in zero to one degrees and we need to be prepared for more such incidents. I have used only a few keywords but, to understand what can happen, the keywords need to be altered or extended for the sake of lucidity. Water is one keyword. The variations of water are river, sea, ocean, glacier, liquid, ice, vapour, snow and so on. If we expand just the word 'sea' with the various possibilities, it could be shipping, water sports, marine engineering, submarine, navy/coast guard, oil spills or the mangroves. One major event happening is the oxygen cylinder issue during Covid times. I had even mentioned gas in the video as water consists of two gases—hydrogen and oxygen. What we need to realise is that if breaking glaciers can lead to floods, lack of rain can lead to drought, and that can lead to a tragedy too. Either way, water will be involved. We can think of a hundred other keywords and all of those could

---

[39] https://www.thehindu.com/news/national/other-states/uttarakhand-glacier-burst/article33798748.ece.

[40] https://www.youtube.com/watch?v=pNU0UP25gmY&t=317s.Z

have possibilities of leading to a major tragedy or a series of small but impactful negative events.

Now, what other things can happen over the next fourteen years of Neptune's stay in Pisces? Lester Brown, a leading environmental scientist, said in 2008 that the shrinking Himalayan glaciers would eventually lead to politically unmanageable food shortage.[41] Now, that was a really serious warning and, if not taken seriously, it could actually become a reality during this period. The paper submitted by Brown suggests that the Himalayan glaciers are receding rapidly, and they could melt entirely by 2035. This period coincides completely with Neptune's stay in Pisces. This is a very real worry, and could impact both India and China, who depend on rivers like the Ganga and the Yellow River.

Neptune will draw focus to maya, the world of make-believe, the showbiz industry. The magic of Neptune will provide a new lease of life to the film industry and the entertainment world. There will be a wave of spiritual awakening too.

I was surprised to read that there are some people who have taken it upon themselves to clean up the oceans.[42] A product line created out of the waste, like sunglasses made from recycled plastics found in the oceans, sounds interesting. During Neptune's stay in Pisces, cleaning the rivers and oceans would become a movement. Neptune would want its water bodies to be cleared of the sins of humans. We must all get together and take some concrete action, beyond the blather and drivel, before it's too late to save the world.

---

[41] Lester R. Brown, 'Melting Mountain Glaciers Will Shrink Grain Harvests in China and India' *Earth Policy Institute*, 20 March 2008, http://www.earth-policy.org/plan_b_updates/2008/update71.

[42] Alice Amundsen, 'From Trash to Treasure: The Ocean Cleanup Story Continues', *Gard*, 20 January 2021, http://www.gard.no/web/updates/content/31068836/from-trash-to-treasure-the-ocean-cleanup-story-continues.

Prediction #3

The Triumvirate Neptune, Pluto and Uranus Bring in Better Times (2022–2024)

Between 2022 and 2024, a rare phenomenon will occur with all the top three planets, Uranus, Neptune and Pluto, entering strong positions. Pluto is already in early exaltation. Add to it the soft and subtle power of Neptune and some potent force of Uranus, and we have a heady combination. It is a combination of innovation (Uranus), transformation (Pluto) and magic (Neptune). Let's look at the areas where this combination can make great things happen.

The world would be slowly coming out of the massive reset caused by Pluto in the form of Covid-19. The second half of 2022 would be the beginning of what we knew as a 'normal' world. Expect the markets to bounce back, economy to boom and a huge boost to the industries in general. The triumvirate of Uranus, Neptune and Pluto will magically push the world towards positive reverberations coming back from the depth of gloom caused by the virus.

Neptune rules spirituality. Expect a burst of spiritual activities around the world. People will now be talking about spiritual emancipation, about the existence of the soul and salvation, and things beyond material possessions. This period will see the rise of spiritual gurus and masters, and they need not necessarily be the conventional ones in robes. Watch out for some events somewhere in the world during this time which will later be classified as miracles. Neptune rules religion and spirituality, but Uranus and Pluto are also present. We need to be wary of some in-fighting within various factions of a religion. This will, over a period of time, lead to some reforms within that religion. We cannot rule out the possibility of communal tensions either. Probably, these problems will eventuality lead to the formation of a new form of religion, religious groups or cult.

Expect humans to conquer water—the seas and the oceans—in a new way. We are running out of drinking water. Expect some viable solutions for that too. Water transport will get a big boost. Even foundations for the building of cities over water could start taking shape. All sorts of innovative, ground-breaking businesses connected with water, oil, vapour, or some other form of liquid or chemicals will be launched and do well. Liquid gold or petrol will be beginning its last lap of significance. Expect other fuels being introduced as substitutes for petrol and its derivatives.

In some corner of the world, a new element, a new metal, or a new alloy may be discovered, which could transform and ease the way many industries work. You can expect a huge new line of industries to be formed due to this discovery or innovation.

Neptune is the natural ruler of the twelfth house. The twelfth house indicates the legs and hence Neptune rules football. It isn't a surprise that when Neptune entered Pisces the last time, in 1857, the next two years saw the establishing of the oldest football clubs in the world like Sheffield FC.[43] Something similar, some kind of innovation or reinvention in football or any other sport connected to the legs, can take place around 2022–2024.

Prediction #4
Pluto in Grey Lizard at 8 to 13 Degrees (2025–2028)
Pluto in Capricorn
Grey Lizard patch

Pluto's presence in the Grey Lizard patch during 2025–2028 will be the worst period for the world, during Pluto's stay in Capricorn. If you thought 2020–2021 was bad, think again. During its nascent entry in Capricorn, Pluto brought back one

---

[43] '9 Oldest Football Clubs in the World', *Oldest.org*, https://www.oldest.org/ sports/football-clubs/, accessed 27 March 2021.

aspect of the Capricornian philosophy—family comes first. In 2019–2021, Pluto made us come back to our families, shrunk our offices hours, and generally made us spend more time at home.

When Pluto enters the Grey Lizard patch, it will probably show the ugly shades of Capricorn. Capricorns, at their worst, can be cunning, scheming, plotting and planning against the enemies—to reach the top positions. Now, when this has to happen at a higher level, involving several countries, then it could mean some negative events involving the battle for supremacy, one-upmanship and territorial conquests.

Don't be surprised if there are some border tensions that even escalate to some wars. Some developed and powerful nations will have skirmishes or civil wars. Looking at the fact that Venus and Mars will be in conjunction many times between 2026 and 2028, these three years may be very vulnerable for world peace. Venus rules peace, and Mars creates conflict and when both come into conjunction, peace is shattered. And if Pluto, the planet of war, is in a Grey Lizard avatar during this patch, it means greater conflicts, huge tensions and, eventually, wars.

One important thing to note here is that the nascent exaltation of Pluto-powered Covid impacted every person in the world. But the Grey Lizard normally doesn't impact everyone. At least this time it won't. That's the reason I feel the tussles and disputes won't escalate to a World War. But those impacted during this period will be affected severely. Wars, destruction, massacres and cruel deaths will dot this period.

One important negative shade of Pluto in Capricorn is to cause some sort of depression. If there is no physical war, there could be trade wars. Post 2008 recession, if there could be a significant market crash, then it will happen during this patch. I'm worried about a huge market crash after a huge high. There could be an artificial 'high' during the preceding years that stems from market manipulations, which could lead to a huge fall during this patch because of its inability to sustain itself. The markets could shrink as the investors turn conservative, which could slow down the economy and lead to more job losses. It could lead to deep depression amongst people. A depressed market leading to a depressed economy further leading to depressed people, could be the outcome of Pluto being in the Grey Lizard patch of Capricorn.

Remember that Neptune is also in its own house during this time, and could add to the confusion. Neptune itself rules tragedy, and the combination with the Grey Lizard Pluto could accentuate this. Neptune's deep magnetic spell could cause some sort of tragedy in water. Shipwrecks, oil spills, marooning, or some other serious environmental hazard due to negligence or abuse of the oceans and other water bodies by human beings could occur. Water wars or wars over water, cities or countries running out of drinking water could be potential issues. Desalinisation of water could lead to some positives and some hazards too. Neptune could also cause some health issues arising out of water or some form of liquid. They could be at either extreme—floods or tsunamis or drought. Earthquakes leading to tsunamis are a possibility, especially after Uranus enters debilitation in Taurus. All these natural calamities will leave parts of the world devastated, causing significant destruction and loss of lives and resources.

Post 2025, Uranus will also be debilitated. If it becomes weak, then there will be no innovation or new ways of solving problems. This period from 2025–2028 will be a patch where the leaders fail to innovate.

Talking about Grey Lizard, many of those who never had major challenges before will now see some huge troubles in life. Watch out for some prominent Grey Lizard personalities born during 1957–1962 to go through some of the biggest setback of their lives.

Are you at that stage in life where you are thinking of starting a family? Should you give birth to a child in this patch?

Pluto in the Grey Lizard avatar will certainly appear in some house of that child's horoscope, and lead to some deep sorrows and troubles in their life. Be it Michael Jackson, Indira Gandhi, Sanjay Dutt or Madonna, no one born in Grey Lizard has had a smooth life. Postpone it, if you can. But a child comes with his or her own destiny and you might be reading this book a bit too late. Let us hope that the child overcomes Pluto's hurdles with the power of Neptune. God bless.

Prediction #5

How the Grey Lizard Will Impact Its Children

Who are the Grey Lizard children? They are those who were born when Pluto was either in exaltation, or in debilitation, from 8 to 13 degrees in that particular zodiac sign. In recent times, Pluto was in exaltation in Leo, and in debilitation in Libra and Sagittarius. It was in the Grey Lizard patch in Leo from late 1957–mid-1962. It was debilitated in Libra during 1984–1986, and in Sagittarius during 2009–2011. These special children have some exceptional karmas to take care of in this lifetime, in some aspect of their lives.

Grey Lizard people go through some extraordinarily tough moments in their lives, or at least one particular moment that brings their world crashing down. They will plunge from the highest high to the lowest low, will stand exposed, or be ravaged by a scandal. They may see death very closely or, worse, be plucked away when their lives seemed all set to soar. They see life from the closest quarters. Sometimes, they have a lifelong regret about what it might have been. Don't be blinded by the glamour, glitz and other frills associated with any of the Grey Lizards. It is not easy living the life of one. I feel sorry for each one of them.

People such as Indira Gandhi and John F. Kennedy paid with their lives. Some could counter a life-altering disease, like

Terry Fox and Michael J. Fox. Some were caught in scandals, like Suresh Kalmadi; some had to face the humiliation of having their integrity questioned, like Kapil Dev. Some, like Emperor Naruhito, had their entire lineage transformed. While some went away too soon, like Malcolm Marshal and Maradona, some took their own lives, like Darby Crash. While some went through a misadventure, like Bruce Lee, some succumbed to a disease, like Rohit Khosla. While some emerged heroes after an incident, like Magic Johnson, some had their career tarnished because of that one incident, like Puneet Issar. While some had to fight their own kin, like Anil Ambani, some had children who would constantly remind the world of their past, like Neena Gupta. Some had to pull their country or state out of their biggest crisis, like Barack Obama and Uddhav Thackeray. There could be a curse on their family, as in the case of John F. Kennedy Jr., or they could offer happiness to all but live a tragic life themselves, like Silk Smitha.

Many well-known Grey Lizards were born during 1984–1986. It is very interesting to see that both Dinesh Karthik and Parthiv Patel were born in the same year—1985! You know their 'Grey Lizard moment'? They were the 'wicket-keeper in waiting' throughout their careers, while M.S. Dhoni stole the show. For Virat Kohli or Lionel Messi it is the pain of waiting for so long to win a trophy that matters, as the captain of their respective countries.

The question now is, have most of the celebrity Grey Lizards already been through their Grey Lizard moments? Most do go through tough moments when Pluto is in a weak position, like when it is in debilitation, or when it is in an opposite state. But what can be worse than Pluto reaching the Grey Lizard patch? It could be the 'moment of truth' for its children.

Harshvardhan Goenka, Andrea Jung, Karan Thapar, Rajkumar Dhoot, Sanjiv Goenka, Nagarjuna, Boman Irani, Mohanlal, Balakrishna, Vadivelu, Venkatesh Daggubati, Suniel

Shetty, Suhasini Maniratnam, Shivrajkumar, Uday Kotak, Gautam Adani, Tom Cruise, Jon Bon Jovi, Garth Brooks, Abdullah II, Shashi Kiran Shetty, Rakesh Jhunjhunwala, Kishore Biyani, Virat Kohli, Harsha Bhogle, Lionel Messi, Emma Thompson, Bryan Adams, Antonio Banderas, Sean Penn, Jean-Claude Van Damme, Eddie Murphy, George Clooney, Ellen DeGeneres, Simon Cowell, Hugh Grant, Antonio Banderas, Madonna, Gary Oldman—the list of those who have not seen any negative impact of their Grey Lizard features, atleast something that the world doesn't know yet, is endless.

The Grey Lizard theory doesn't apply only to human beings, but to businesses too. Lehmann Brothers was established during a Grey Lizard patch and shut down in another. So did Blockbuster. Sometimes, a company like Enron, which was founded during a debilitated Grey Lizard Pluto patch, went down when Pluto was in a strong position. The point is that organisations, too, are afflicted by the Grey Lizard syndrome. Those established during certain years need to be extra careful during this approaching Grey Lizard patch. And investors need to stay away from these companies. We will talk about these organisations and the respective years in prediction #17.

There are some exceptions to this rule, though. People who are in uniformed services—such as the army, navy, police, secret services—or sports people, and people who have any connections to alternative practices like wizardry and magic will not be impacted much by the Grey Lizard patch. These people live on the edge all the time or their careers themselves are full of challenges, disappointments or tragedy, anyway.

Prediction #6
Pluto Moving Towards 25 Degrees in Capricorn (2029–2038)

I am pretty excited about this long run of Pluto in Capricorn post the Grey Lizard patch. The power of Pluto in its unadulterated and positive form, the soft and soothing energy of Neptune, and Uranus just getting into nascent exaltation in the mischievous Gemini, all add up to a heady mix. This may lead to one of the best periods in a long time to come.

As the saying goes, when you have reached the rock bottom, the only way is the way up. During the rule of the Grey Lizard, the world reaches the bottom. Everything that can go wrong, does. Huge problems occur during this phase. This leads to the depths of despair. Anything after this Grey Lizard patch can only be better. This time the spring-back will be even more dramatic because Neptune and Uranus, too, will be in powerful positions.

Pluto will focus on growth in career and the workspace as it is still in Capricorn. Expect industries to boom, job markets to improve, and salaries to skyrocket. There will be improvement in happiness and the general well-being of humankind. As Pluto has positive energy now, and has already accomplished status and power after a huge fight, it doesn't need to fight for the top position anymore, because it's already there. There will be fewer fights between countries, fewer power struggles, and more peace.

Neptune will be in a position to exert its positive energy as there will be no Grey Lizard to curb its natural flow. Uranus will also be positive. Neptune will bestow its most valuable gift to humankind—peace. There will be harmony, people will be more spiritually self-aware, and there will be less confusions and delusions. The stock markets will grow steadily and hit new highs. This is the period when you can really plan your wealth-creation activities. There will be fewer chances for you to lose money in any kind of a sudden fall during this phase than in any other phase of Pluto in Capricorn.

This will be a period of expansion. Industries will grow and mature. There will be large-scale development everywhere, and very high growth in every sector you can envisage. The positivity of each sector will spill over into the others and push them to do well.

Uranus in Gemini will bring in new energy and playfulness into the entire equation. People will be more relaxed and will have fun. There will be greater permissiveness in the society. New avenues and ways of entertainment, fun, happiness, peace and prosperity will mark this decade. I should go on to say that this decade could be compared to the roaring 1920s and you could call it the roaring 2030s.

Economists talk about peaks, troughs and plateaus in economic cycles. Astrologically, this would be the period when it goes from trough to peak. This entire happy period will start from 2029 and reach its acme by around 2038.

Prediction #7
Some Magic You Can Plan and Use
April 2022 to March 2024
November 2031 to September 2032
January 2036 to February 2037

Being an astrologer, one of the most frequent requests I receive is from people desperate enough to pay me any amount of money for information about an auspicious date and time for their pregnant wife's delivery so that their child can go on to be rich and famous. Some even throw names like Sachin Tendulkar, Shah Rukh Khan or Barack Obama, and even combinations of two or more names.

I have a hearty laugh at those situations. Sachin Tendulkar was born when Uranus was in deep exaltation with Pluto in conjunction. This phenomenon occurs once in about 250 years. Shah Rukh Khan was born when Neptune, Pluto and Chiron were at their deepest exaltation points simultaneously. It will take another 250 years for this phenomenon to occur again. Such prominent personalities, who make a mark in this world, are born during those extraordinary moments when the planets are in extremely rare combinations, and that is why their achievements are so rare. Therefore, if you want to give birth to another Shah Rukh Khan, you'll need to wait for another 250 years.

Sometimes, people also ask me for an opportune moment to set up their business so that it becomes another Microsoft or Reliance. The same factors apply here too. Microsoft, Reliance and Amazon were formed during extraordinary moments in time. Such mega-successes cannot be started in any random year.

Do you need to wait for another 250 years to have a shot at giving birth to another great baby, or start a great organisation? No, you don't need to. Some rare combinations do come along sometimes, and we are really lucky that we have three such moments happening in the next twenty years. I know that's a pretty long time-frame but, just in case you have long-term plans, or are reading this book at the right time, you can go ahead.

The lucky ones among you may have a child or start their own organisation during these times. But, mind you, each child comes with their own unique life plan, based on their past life karmas. There is a possibility that the child may be born with these important planets, in not-so-important quadrants, and the child may not turn out to be a great personality after all. But, in case you really want to make a difference and start doing something significant that will last a long time, then you should try these years. Obviously, you need to 'time' the events with the help of a professional astrologer to make it more specific to you.

The three astrologically significant patches are:

1. April 2022 to March 2024

Uranus will be in exaltation in Aries and will be slowly moving towards deep exaltation, Neptune will be in nascent exaltation and Pluto, too, will be in exaltation before it enters the Grey Lizard patch. Uranus, Neptune and Pluto coming into 'dignified' positions simultaneously is a rare event, and this phenomenon will stay for almost two years. See how well you can use it.

2. November 2031 to September 2032

This is one phenomenal period. This kind of a period comes perhaps twice or at the most thrice in a millennium. All the planets beyond Jupiter, including even Uranus, Neptune and Pluto, are in dignity and will be either in exaltation or in their own house. That's really extraordinary! Besides Jupiter and Saturn, all the four centaurs—Planet-X, Planet-Y, Planet-Z and Chiron, will also be also be in dignity. Uranus and Pluto will be reaching their deepest exaltation points, while Neptune will be in its own house. That is a phenomenal arrangement of the planets. To tell you how big it is, Microsoft was formed when all the four centaurs were in the strongest positions. Reliance was formed when Neptune and Pluto were in deepest exaltation. *This* period is like a combination of the two—Microsoft plus Reliance. Some of the greatest organisations, and some of the greatest people, will be born at this time. Do you think *you* may have a chance in making it happen?

3. January 2036 to February 2037

This is a patch when Pluto and Uranus will simultaneously be in deep exaltation and Neptune will be about to exit its last lap of dignity in its own house. This is almost equivalent to the 'Shah Rukh Khan' patch—well, almost.

Twenty years on from that point, you will know that some of the biggest organisations and some of the greatest people were born during these patches.

My best wishes for you to make the best use of this period!

Prediction #8
Economic Indices to Watch from 2021 to 2040

How we all wish we knew which industry will go up and which will come down before it actually happened! Fund managers sieve through volumes of data and run through hundreds of algorithms to arrive at the industry or the company they are going to invest in. Astrology has its own algorithms to do that. If you understand them well and in the right way, they can be much more reliable than any other forecasting tool.

Different economic factors are ruled by different planets. The interplays of these planets determine how a particular commodity or an industry performs. While Uranus, Neptune and Pluto govern the larger aspects of how the world goes forward, smaller bodies like Chiron have their own important roles to play.

When a planet enters its dignified position, the industry connected with it does well, and the opposite happens when the planet goes into fall or debilitation. At the same time, do not forget that everything is subject to Pluto's control. Pluto is the big boss, and the larger perspective on that period is governed by Pluto. However, the smaller planets do hold value and shine, despite the major planets in challenging positions. This probably indicates the dichotomy of any situation in life and also of the stock markets.

Let me give you an example of how this works. Let's say Pluto has gone into debilitation or into a Grey Lizard patch. At that same time, Chiron is in exaltation. So what would be the result? Pluto would result in devastation and hurly-burly. Let us say there is a war. Chiron rules real estate. Consequently, after the destruction of a city, post-war reconstruction would happen and the real estate industry would thrive.

We have already looked at what the planets stand for in the chapter 'Pluto Creates the Cycles'. Now we can see the zodiac signs in which the planets will be and in what state, so that we can plan our future finances and investments for the next twenty years. Here:

- Exalted/Own house means positive for the sectors indicated by the planet.
- Debilitated/Fall means negative for the sectors indicated by the planet.
- Neutral means not much of action or a plateau phase.

Pluto: 2019 October to March 2039—Exalted in Capricorn

Neptune: April 2022 to February 2037—In own house, Pisces

Uranus: Until May 2024—Exalted in Aries; June 2024 to June 2031—Debilitated in Taurus; July 2031 to July 2038—Exalted in Gemini

Planet-Y: April 2021 to December 2023—Exalted in Scorpio; January 2024 to December 2027—Debilitated in Sagittarius; January 2028 to January 2030—Exalted in Capricorn; February 2030 to April 2033—Exalted in Aquarius; May 2033 to May 2035—Fall in Pisces; June 2035 to June 2038—Exalted in Aries

Planet-X: Until May 2022—In own house in Taurus; June 2023 to July 2035—Exalted in Gemini; August 2035 to July 2043—Exalted in Cancer

Planet-Z: Until August 2022—Debilitated in Gemini; September 2022 to September 2026—Debilitated in Cancer; October 2026 to August 2033—In own house, Leo; September 2033 to October 2039—Debilitated in Virgo

Chiron: Until February 2026—Debilitated in Pisces; April 2026 to May 2033—Exalted in Aries; June 2033 to July 2037—Debilitated in Taurus; August 2037 to July 2041—Debilitated in Gemini

Here is an example of how to use this. Planet-Y entered into exaltation in November 2020. It is the ruler of Virgo. Virgo corresponds to everything connected with the sixth house. One of the main indicators of the sixth house is health. Which industry corresponds to health? Pharmaceuticals. What happened just when Planet-Y entered into exaltation? Vaccines for Covid were launched. Obviously, the pharma industry will do well in the next couple of years. It's time to invest in pharma. Had you invested in it in anticipation of the upcoming exaltation of Planet-Y, you would have reaped big rewards.

This is an over-simplified example. Financial astrology is deep and vast. There are multiple exaltation and debilitation points for a planet and each of them will produce different kinds of results. The scope of this book doesn't allow us to dive deeply into them. But you can apply the basic principle and explore your own ideas using these indices.

Mercury, Venus and Mars are very minor bodies and keep moving frequently and result in minor fluctuations daily in the stock market. Jupiter and Saturn are slightly more important, and they indicate the current trend. But the planets starting from Chiron up to Pluto are the most important, and control the theme of that industry during a particular period.

The minor bodies can be used for day trading, but if you really want to make a fortune or create wealth, then you need to look at a longer time horizon—and that's exactly what Chiron and planets beyond it provide. If you are a financial planner, then you certainly need to have a plan for Pluto and its allies.

Prediction #9
What Is the Future of Cryptocurrencies?

Paul Krugman, winner of the 2008 Nobel Prize in Economic Sciences, has repeated numerous times that cryptocurrencies are a bubble that will not last, and links them to Tulip mania.[44]

---

[44] Jacqui Frank, Kara Chin and Joe Ciolli, 'Paul Krugman: Bitcoin Is a More Obvious Bubble Than Housing Was', *Business Insider*, 15 December 2017, https://www.businessinsider.in/stock-market/paul-krugman-bitcoin-is-a-more-obvious-bubble-than-housing-was/articleshow/62088616.cms.

American business magnate and investment guru, Warren Buffett, thinks that cryptocurrency will come to a bad end.[45] Both these gentlemen will prove to be right. Cryptocurrencies, especially the earliest ones, will face a bad end.

To give a background, Bitcoin and all cryptocurrencies are digital forms of a currency that can be used to buy goods and services, but use an online ledger with strong cryptography to secure online transactions. The most important thing to know about them is that they are not regulated by most countries and are susceptible to frauds. Tulip Mania was a period during the Dutch Golden Age when contract prices for some bulbs of the recently introduced and fashionable tulip reached extraordinarily high levels, and then dramatically collapsed in February 1637.

Bitcoin was launched in January 2009, a few months after the 2008 economic meltdown. In the period between 2008 and 2009, the two most powerful planets in the universe, Neptune and Pluto, went into deep debilitation. This happens very rarely. Pluto rules over people's money and financial institutions—in fact, all forms of transactions of money, both legal and illegal. Planet-X rules money, and everything money can buy.

Neptune, at its best, indicates beauty and magic and, at its worst, creates deception, deceit and confusion. If you need to associate any planet with the word 'bubble', then it has to be Neptune. A bubble is an illusion that appears to be true, but isn't so. It may grow into something huge, but it is just a matter of time before it bursts. Tulip Mania,[46] one of the legendary financial bubbles economists talk about, started when Neptune was in deep exaltation in the mid-1630s, and burst in 1637, when Neptune reached its debilitation point.

---

[45] 'Warren Buffett: Cryptocurrency Will Come to a Bad Ending', *CNBC*, 10 January 2018, https://www.cnbc.com/video/2018/01/10/warren-buffett-cryptocurrency-will-come-to-a-bad-ending.html.

[46] Mike Dash, *Tulipomania: The Story of the World's Most Coveted Flower & the Extraordinary Passions It Aroused* (Crown, 2001).

Besides Tulip Mania, whenever there has been a financial bubble anywhere in the world, Neptune has always been the culprit. At the time of Bitcoin's launch, Neptune was in deep debilitation, indicating very clearly that cryptocurrencies, specifically Bitcoin, was going to be a huge bubble which will burst one day. And that day is not too far away. This is exactly the opposite of the case of Tulip Mania. Tulip Mania started when Neptune was exalted, and burst when Neptune entered debilitation. Cryptocurrencies, on the other hand, started when Neptune was in deep debilitation, and will burst when Neptune reaches its own house—as the forces are opposite to one another.

Neptune is also associated with frauds and deceptions. It is no surprise that many cryptocurrency start-ups have gone bankrupt, and some of them have been associated with fraudulent Ponzi schemes. There are cases where the currencies have been hacked, involved in wire frauds, locked in, stolen, phished or hashed.[47]

One of the reasons why Bitcoin has fascinated people is because its technology is very mysterious and considered to be very strong. The very assumption that this technology is impregnable could prove to be a mirage as Bitcoin was designed during the influence of a negative Neptune. The CEO of the microblogging site Twitter has tied up with Jay-Z, rapper and investor, to augment Bitcoin development in India and African countries.[48] But this endeavour will not bear fruits in the long run.

The Chinese government has already started working on its own official digital currency and India, too, will follow suit

---

[47] Conrad Barski and Chris Wilmer, *Bitcoin for the Befuddled* (No Starch Press, 2014).

[48] Ankita Chakravarti, 'Twitter CEO Jack Dorsey, Jay-Z Collaborate for Bitcoin Endowment', *India Today*, 13 February 2021, https://www.indiatoday.in/technology/news/story/-twitter-ceo-jack-dorsey-jay-z-collaborate-for-bitcoin-endowment-1768905-2021-02-13.

soon.[49] A set of new digital currencies, in new avatars, will come up during the 2020s, which would be far more superior and safer, transparent and universally accepted. And that will bring the entire saga of the earlier versions of cryptocurrencies to an end. Yes, from the family of cryptocurrencies or whatever they would be called in future, only those floated during the 2020s will survive. All the initial versions launched during 2008–2018 will meet their gradual end. The grand old man of financial investments, Warren Buffett, will once again be proved right.

Prediction #10

Is This the End of Oil?

Oil was commercially extracted for the first time in 1859 by Colonel Drake. No prizes for guessing which planet was in the strongest position at that point of time—Neptune, of course. Neptune came to its own house, and was in the nascent stage, when the discovery and the extraction happened. In 2022, Neptune will come back to the same position where it was when oil was discovered for the first time. As the cycle for oil is complete, it will find it difficult to push its importance further in the times ahead.

Many countries have adopted strategies to bring down the production and dependence on fossil fuels. India aims to increase the share of non-fossil fuels to 40 per cent of total electricity-generation capacity by 2030.[50] More countries will follow suit.

But will oil be completely replaced by something else immediately or in the near future? No, I don't think so. It won't

---

[49]   Andy Mukherjee, 'India Has a Backdoor Entry into Digital Currency. Will It Take It?', *The Economic Times*, 10 February 2021, https://economictimes.indiatimes.com/markets/stocks/news/india-has-a-backdoor-entry-into-digital-currency-will-it-take-it/articleshow/80778774.cms.

[50]   Srinivasa Rao Patnana, 'Energy Transition in India: Move Towards Self-Reliance and Sustainability', *KPMG*, 20 November 2020, https://home.kpmg/in/en/home/insights/2020/11/energy-transition-in-india.html.

be that fast. As the world slowly moves towards electric, solar and other forms of renewable energy sources, oil will still stay relevant as there are many industries, other than transport, which also use oil. The question is, how long will oil consumption last? As long as Neptune stays in its own house, that is, till 2036. Petrol won't be liquid gold in 2036.

A look at the horoscopes of some of the heads of the countries whose economies depend mainly on oil will give an idea of how things will pan out in the future.[51] Saudi Arabia is the largest exporter of oil. Prince Mohammed bin Salman, the future king of the country, was born in 1985. He is a Grey Lizard with Pluto in deepest debilitation. Pluto will be in exaltation for at least the next half-century. The most important planet is exactly opposite the forces in the horoscope of the Prince. This means that, under his rule, the country will only decline. Saudi Arabia's economy depends heavily on oil. The privatisation of the state-owned oil company, Aramco, and the reforms announced by the Prince to prepare for a future less dependent on oil, will push the country's economy to do well in other areas, but if his horoscope is a clear indicator, he won't be able to prevent the slide.

Countries where fuel accounts for more than 90 per cent of their total exports include Algeria, Azerbaijan, Brunei Darussalam, Iraq, Kuwait, Libya, Sudan and Venezuela. They are also either led by people who have weak horoscopes, or will be succeeded by people who have weak ones. The horoscopes of Prince Salman and others clearly indicate that the future of oil is negative.

I wouldn't be surprised if some other materials are discovered that replace oil and its derivatives over a period of time. Some other cheaper, better, renewable and easier to use options could be discovered or 'rediscovered', probably during

---

51   Rosamond Hutt, 'Which Economies Are Most Reliant on Oil?' *World Economic Forum*, 10 May 2016, https://www.weforum.org/agenda/2016/05/ which-economies-are-most-reliant-on-oil/.

2031 or around that time. When all the three major bodies—Uranus, Neptune and Pluto—become stronger simultaneously, such a future-altering event could happen.

Prediction #11
Will Carbon Emissions Ever Reduce?

Do you believe in reincarnation? I do. I truly believe that the quality of our present life is a consequence of our karmas in our past lives. Do you think you will be born again? I do. I don't have any apprehensions about being born in this world again. The only scary image that used to haunt me was of human beings walking around with masks and portable cylinder due to the overwhelming pollution.

We discussed the future of oil in the last chapter. The crux here is—it is not just about oil. Carbon emission comes from a number of sources, not simply vehicles. I had never imagined that even agriculture could create carbon and other harmful emissions. [52]

Melting glaciers, rising sea levels, droughts, forest fires, drying lakes, changes in flora and fauna are some of the other frightening consequences of carbon emissions and the consequent global warming. The only way this can be controlled is through the collective efforts of all the countries. The Paris Agreement in 2015, signed by 184 countries, was a good beginning. [53]

While it may be impossible to bring the carbon emission levels down to zero, reaching a level where all products and services comply with the carbon emission norms will be compulsory in the future. Capricorn, the father, is aware of what is good for his home, and implements the same. The next

---

[52] https://www.nationalgeographic.com/environment/article/global-warming-overview.

[53] Mayank Aggarwal, 'India Needs to Double Rate of Forest Cover Expansion to Achieve Paris Agreement Target', *Mongabay*, 6 November 2019, https://india.mongabay.com/2019/11/paris-agreement-goals-india-needs-to-double-forest-cover-expansion-rate/.

twenty years will be more about implementing the rules and, in this case, they will be regarding carbon emissions.

The most exciting thing about the next fifty years is that Pluto is going to remain exalted. Pluto's exaltation means more innovations, transformations, research and realignment. Also, it will move from Capricorn into Aquarius, and then finally into Pisces. Capricorn will look at the economies of scale, the viability of fuel consumption and the impact upon economies and livelihoods. When Pluto enters Aquarius, post 2039, the world will see the dawn of a new era, a new way of working. From 2040, the next two decades will be all about transforming how we will live on this planet. Expect the world to change for the better. Solar energy, reduced carbon emissions, renewable energy, sustainable energy, eco-friendly resources—these will be some of the key themes. With Pluto in Aquarius, we will find some innovative ways to reduce carbon emissions. In the forty years after that as Pluto enters Pisces and Aries, Pisces would keep up the good work and Aries would enhance it.

If solar energy is the way to go, then we will figure out the ways to harness it. If building cities on water works better, then we may venture in that direction. If finding an alternative fuel is the solution, then we will ensure we find it. Neptune will also be exalted in this patch, and it will ensure the solutions are found, whether in liquid form or something else.

Yes, contrary to what some experts tell you, our children won't inherit a dark, damp, fuel-less world, after all. And then, I wouldn't mind coming back to this earth once again.

Prediction #12
How Pluto Will Impact Some Countries

Do countries have birth charts? Yes, they do!
New countries are formed if they become independent, if they attain democracy or become a republic, or if there is a massive

change in their constitution, or if there are huge realignments in their geographical features due to natural forces like glacier meltdowns. For Pakistan, it was the first case, while for Russia it was the last one.

Whenever new countries are formed, the planets at the horizon indicate the kind of future they will have. There are Grey Lizard countries born when Pluto is in 8–13 degrees of exaltation or debilitation. Nascent or deep exaltation is equally applicable to countries. When a country goes through some major restructuring, the fortunes of the country change too. Let's look at how some countries will fare in the next twenty to thirty years, when Pluto is in exaltation and Neptune, too, remains powerful.

India attained independence at midnight on 15 August in 1947, when Pluto was in debilitation in Cancer. And, unfortunately, it was an amavasya day as well! This resulted in some of the darkest moments in the history of India—the Partition. The massacres and displacement of millions was due to this single factor.

Thankfully for India, she became a Republic on an extraordinary day in 1950, when Pluto was in nascent exaltation and Uranus and Saturn were in deep exaltation. It was almost like a rebirth. The actual governance of the country started then, and that is why we take it as India's date of birth.

There is no question about the fact that India will go on to become a superpower. India currently boasts of one of the youngest populations in the world. It is all set to grow phenomenally in the next half century. Some people ask me the question, when India and Pakistan became independent on the same day, why are their economic and other indices so vastly different? Well, the answer lies in what the countries did after that. India became a Republic on 26 January 1950 and Pakistan became an Islamic Republic on 23 March 1956. If you compare the dates, the day of India's becoming a republic has much stronger planetary positions compared to Pakistan's. Another country that was carved out of Pakistan was Bangladesh. Watch out for this younger nation. The 1971-born country has better planets than Pakistan and will grow quicker.

There are demands that India should be renamed as Bharat. I have no opinion about the religious or patriotic reasons behind this, but if India is to be renamed, I would urge the leaders not to do so during 2025–2028. If it is done before 2025, or maybe sometime in the later years—post 2028—there could be another dash of luck for India.

One country that will remain better than India for many years, if not for a century, is China. China has a better horoscope than India, and will continue to do well. There is another country which became independent around the same time as India and China, and will show the fastest growth in the next half century—Indonesia.

And there are some Grey Lizard and Pluto-in-debilitation countries, which will not do very well in the future, irrespective of how well they are doing now. Iran and Saudi Arabia are two such countries. A few countries may show a surprising slide in the next half century—France, Italy, South Korea and Japan. France is a Grey Lizard, and South Korea, Italy and Japan have a debilitated Pluto. Japan will have the greatest fall amongst all. There is one country whose potential the economists underestimate, and it will do better than what is expected of it—Canada.

Here is a list of the top twenty countries in the world, their 'birth date' and a few other important years and how things will pan out for them in the future:

1. Australia—1788/1901/9 October 1942: Despite everything the land promises, it will face some huge obstacles and roadblocks in the future. However, the country should grow and do well despite them.
2. Brazil—1822/15 November 1889: There is tremendous scope for growth at a fast clip now.

3. Canada—1 July 1867/1982: It is a sleeping giant. It will slowly wake up and start running in the next fifteen years.

4. China—1 October 1949: It has one of the best planetary positions. It will continue to dominate the world.

5. England—1 January 1801: It has lived its glory to the full. Now it will slowly start fading in significance. If they reinvent themselves in their better years, there may be chances of a revival.

6. France—22 September 1792: It needs to reinvent itself, or it will gradually lose out to the newer countries.

7. Germany—3 October 1990: It has great energy. It may be small in size, but it will make a huge impact.

8. India—1947/26 January 1950: India will grow tremendously, despite huge political and other complications.

9. Indonesia—27 December 1949: It will probably be the fastest growing country in the next half century.

10. Italy—6 June 1946: A past glory. The downward slide begins here.

11. Japan—3 May 1947: It has loads of troubles ahead. It may keep slipping despite all efforts. It will need some serious resurrection; the days of glory may be over.

12. Mexico—5 February 1917: It will face issues with its economy and standards of living despite its good growth.

13. Russia—12 December 1991: It will grow tremendously, and with an open culture.

14. Saudi Arabia—23 September 1932: A declining power.

15. South Africa—27 April 1994: It will become one of the top twenty countries, and will grow fast.

16. South Korea—17 July 1948: It needs to reinvent itself, or it will fade into oblivion.

17. Spain—29 December 1978: It will have to fight hard to stay as a top country.

18. Switzerland—12 September 1848: It will be stable, but there aren't many growth factors.
19. Turkey—29 October 1923: It will show a decent amount of growth in the coming years.
20. United States—7 July 1776: The country will largely maintain its dominance, and continue to be the dream destination. India and China will push to compete with the USA in the coming years. The three countries together will be the three power centres of the world.

Prediction #13
Country Rankings in 2035

Seeing any kind of a scoreboard really makes me excited. It probably has something to do with being a salesperson in my early years. This scoreboard should be of interest to many. According to International Monetary Fund, the top twenty countries in terms of GDP in PPP (Purchasing Power Parity) terms in the year 2020 are as follows:

1. USA, 2. China, 3. Japan, 4. Germany, 5. India, 6. United Kingdom, 7. France, 8. Italy, 9. Brazil, 10. Canada, 11. Russia, 12. South Korea, 13. Spain, 14. Australia, 15. Mexico, 16. Indonesia, 17. Netherlands, 18. Saudi Arabia, 19. Turkey, 20. Switzerland.

There hasn't been much change in the top twenty in the last forty years, except in the positions of the last three. Countries like Sweden, Belgium and Austria have been playing catch-up with Saudi Arabia, Turkey and Switzerland.

Assuming that these top twenty will remain where they are in the next fifteen years, let us see how the world economy will look in terms of the GDP in PPP in 2035. The astrological data considered is the date of birth of the country. It could be either the date of its independence, or the date when it became a democracy or a republic.

There are several economy-ranking syndicates that offer projections for the ranking of the world economy in the future. Here I've used one of the best available source—CEBR (Centre for Economics and Business Research), based in the UK. CEBR has used several economic indices to arrive at this list.[54] In our case, we have utilised the planetary strengths of the countries to arrive at the rankings. When compared with CEBR, we cannot agree more that China will overtake the United States as the largest economy in the world. A very fast-growing India will be in the third position. Probably by 2050, India would even overtake the United States.

Ranking	2021 Ranking by CEBR	2035 Ranking by CEBR	2035 Ranking by astrology
1	United States	China	China
2	China	United States	United States
3	Japan	India	India
4	Germany	Japan	Germany
5	United Kingdom	Germany	United Kingdom
6	India	United Kingdom	Indonesia
7	France	France	Brazil
8	Italy	Indonesia	Japan
9	Canada	Brazil	Russia
10	Korea	Russia	France

54 'World Economic League Table 2021', *Cebr*, December 2020, https://cebr.com/wp-content/uploads/2020/12/WELT-2021-final-23.12.pdf.

Watch out for the other country that came into being around the same time as India and China—Indonesia. This country will push its way into the top ten, and grow further.

There are two countries in the top ten which will, astrologically, find it hard to stay there for long. They are Japan and France. Though both these countries will still be in the top ten in 2035, it will only be a matter of time before they slip down. In 2035, I expect Germany and United Kingdom to have pushed themselves up a bit. While Germany will actively push itself, the UK will maintain its position, as Japan and France witness a collapse.

Russia and Brazil are expected to do very well, and I believe they will. I do expect Brazil and Russia to be in the top ten by 2035. Canada doesn't feature in the top ten of CEBR either. I have given the number ten position to France. It's only a matter of time before France slips out of top ten, and Canada comes back into the reckoning in the 2040s. This can happen even by late 2030s. Canada has a fantastic horoscope and I feel that, despite the growth of many Asian countries, Canada will be able to float around the ten to twelve position. Does that have anything to do with the huge population of immigrants from Asia? Maybe.

While I agree that the UK and France may slide down slowly from the top ten, I wouldn't say the same about Germany. The current United Germany and Russia were formed around the same time, and have a similar set of planets. They will remain in the top ten even in 2035. Perhaps the larger size of the country, a better exploitation of natural resources and a growing population will be the reasons for Russia's growth beyond Germany, in the 2040s.

We also need to be aware of the fact that the pecking order may change under a few circumstances—if a country's governance is redefined, or if its borders change, or if a new country attains independence or loses it, or if there is a change in the sovereignty. Though Russia has been around for long, its birth is considered to be 1991, after the USSR collapsed. West and East Germany combined forces in 1990. Similar collapses or mergers cannot be ruled out in the future, and that will alter the fortunes of the country and its ranking, and would impact other countries too.

Prediction #14
Pluto in Capricorn: Biggest Impact upon India

Every country can be assigned a zodiac sign. The Japanese, who seem to be meticulous, health conscious and attentive to small details, can be considered as Virgos. Americans are very progressive, technology-based, open and frank, a bit aloof when it comes to relationships, so maybe we can assign Aquarius to them. I don't consider this form of classification for any predictions about India, or any nation for that matter, but if at all you do, then, yes, we can assign Capricorn to India. India, with its rich cultural heritage, value systems and a strong emphasis on relationships and family, does resonate more with it.

With Pluto in Capricorn for the next twenty years, we have talked about how certain Capricorn traits, both progressive and regressive, could be heightened. Probably, all of this started already when Pluto was in Sagittarius between 2006 and 2020. One of the things Sagittarius rules is religion and spirituality. Religion and spirituality came into focus during that time, but for the wrong reasons. We witnessed a kind of religious uprising and fanaticism. Many incidents highlighted the conflicts simmering within the country, based on different religious belief systems. There were even talks about religious intolerance. In 2017, a Pew Research Centre analysis of most populous countries ranked India amongst the worst in the world for religious intolerance.[55] The Pew Research Centre

---

[55] Murali Krishnan, 'India's Intolerance Is Hurting the Country', *The Interpreter*, 2 February 2018, https://www.lowyinstitute.org/the-interpreter/indias-intolerance-hurting-country.

examined various hate crimes—communal violence, religion-related terror, the use of force to prevent religious practice, the harassment of women for not conforming to religious dress codes, and violence over conversion or proselytising.

Sagittarius is all about speaking fearlessly, but when Pluto was in debilitation, that freedom was threatened. In 2017, a documentary, *The Argumentative Indian* based on a book of the same name by Nobel Laureate, Amartya Sen, faced much controversy before it was screened, as it contained certain words against the political party in power at the Centre? There have been repeated incidents of threats, murders, lynching, banning and burning of books. The hatred towards members of other religions, pointing a finger at someone's identity based on the person's religion, started growing during the phase.

Pakistani singer Ghulam Ali was forced to cancel his concert in India. A major publishing house withdrew all copies of *The Hindus: An Alternative History* by US-based academic, Wendy Doniger.

When Pluto was in Sagittarius, all the finger-pointing, the accusations, and the difficulties were confrontational. But Pluto moved into Capricorn in 2020. Now expect everything to be subtly masterminded. Capricorn is a zodiac sign that believes in the traditional, old-fashioned values. Capricorns believe whatever their ancestors practised was right, whether or not it was actually so. Through the next twenty years, when Pluto is in Capricorn, expect India to go back to her roots. Or rather, I should say, it will be made to go back several centuries. Certain people, who believe that the old way of doing things was the right way to do them, will want to impose their views on others in the modern times too. This could be a regressive Capricorn syndrome which we will witness in the coming times.

The regressive mindsets will also influence the education system, lifestyle, food habits and everything we say and do. Expect mythology to be revered, heroic historical figures to be venerated. You will constantly be told that it is the right way ahead, because our ancestors did that. There would be curbs on media and the news that finally reaches you would be doctored and there would be clever manipulations of opinions. Mind you, this entire phenomenon will play out very subtly, maybe even in a non-violent way, since there is no Sagittarius involved now. It will be stage-managed so beautifully that you won't even realise how it happened.

Will there be any good that comes out of this? Definitely. India is a country with a rich heritage, and many hidden gems will find their place under the sun. Expect traditional sciences, such as yoga, meditation, Ayurveda, and even astrology, to receive a boost. The downside of this may be that if the approach is not scientific, then many quacks will peddle superstition and untruths. There will also be a planned control of modern ideas and systems that may not be allowed to flourish, or implemented, on the basis that they are foreign or alien. There will be control and distinction on the basis of religion, belief systems, tradition and culture. This is the kind of conservatism Pluto in Capricorn will bring in India.

Sometimes, astrological predictions can be plain common sense.

Prediction #15
When Will India and Pakistan Be at Peace?

When I asked some friends the most important question they wanted answered in my book of predictions, apart from when Salman Khan would get married, the majority asked when there would be peace between India and Pakistan. This shows that most people want peace. If you are a common person, you may have wondered several times why all these powerful leaders in the past, or the leaders of today, cannot resolve this tension simmering between the two countries, initiate a peace dialogue, and be friendly towards each other. Why wasn't peace ever given a chance?

India and Pakistan probably stayed in a state of conflict due to some vested interests. There were elections to be won, movies to be made, wars to be waged and won, patriotism to be stoked and fanned, products to be sold, above all, military equipment worth billions of dollars to be sold. Otherwise, people visiting the other country have always been surprised by how the people there, too, want only peace, and how they entertain and regale them when they're there. Pakistan is being projected as a living hell on earth. Perhaps, on the other side, the Pakistanis believe the same thing about India. Only the Indians and Pakistanis living in far-off Canada or UAE laugh at the silliness of this whole political game.

Will there ever be peace between the two countries? Yes, certainly. When? Well, it cannot happen until the most liberal amongst the zodiac—Aquarius—signs appears over the horizon.

Pluto will transit into the friendly Aquarius in 2040, and will stay there till 2064. This could be the phase when brotherhood is given a chance. Aquarius is the most tolerant and the most liberal amongst all the zodiac signs. Aquarians believe in friendship and in the dictum of 'live and let live'. Aquarians have a broader outlook, and better tolerance and acceptance of people who are unlike them. They are excited by and welcome diversity in everything. They don't look at people from the perspective of region or religion, and usually work towards the betterment of the society.

In the late 2030s, there will be some movement initiated by some young leaders who believe in brotherhood, harmonious coexistence and peace. These leaders from either side of the border will initiate the process, and then both the sides would mutually ensure that there is harmony between the two countries. Remember, sometimes even peace has to be bought by war. There could be some mini-battles, fights and insurgencies which will have to be quelled before peace is made possible, and brotherhood is established. The leaders who bring in this enormous change would have been born at the turn of the twenty-first century.

One day, you or your offspring will be able to visit Pakistan without worrying about spending the rest of your life in an obscure jail. Maybe one day you won't even require a visa to go there. There will be a trade-and-business relationship with your the friendly neighbour. It looks like a distant dream at present, but it is undoubtedly a possibility when Pluto enters the humanitarian and brotherly Aquarius. There were tears during the Partition, and now there will be happy tears when there is peace.

Prediction #16
Will India and China Go to War?

The skirmishes on the Line of Actual Control (LAC) between India and China have raised an alarm about the possibility of a war. Will this really escalate into another war similar to the one in 1962?

Highly unlikely.

The Sino-Indian war of 1962 lasted for just about a month. This happened when Pluto was exalted in the Grey Lizard avatar. The then prime minister of India, Jawaharlal Nehru, had a debilitated Uranus transiting into his twelfth house of hidden enemies, and the war ensued. But the war didn't last long, as the planet involved was relatively minor. If Pluto had been involved, the results would have been devastating.

Considering 2021, Pluto is yet to go into the Grey Lizard avatar. It will do so only in 2025. If at all there is any possibility of a war, it can only happen in 2025 or later. But the chances of that seem very little, because of a particular planetary position in the horoscope of the Indian prime minister. Modi has the transiting Pluto exalted in his fourth house. It is his second lord getting exalted in the fourth house. The second house means finance, the fourth house refers to the country of birth, or the motherland, and internal affairs. This implies Modi's focus will be entirely on nation-building, and on improving the situation of the economy in his country. The focus will be inwards and not outwards. This seems obvious after Covid-19, since it has significantly weakened the economy of the country. And Modi seems to have begun the process of rebuilding the economy.

During 2016–2019, when Planet-X was in his eighth house, Modi engaged the Indian forces in some surgical strikes in select locations in Pakistan.[56] The eighth house indicates war, and Planet-X is placed there right now. However, Planet-X is a minor body compared to Pluto. Surgical strikes cannot be called wars, and a few border skirmishes will not escalate into a war. Had Pluto been transiting the eighth house, we would have been talking about something different, something more disturbing. Now we can breathe in peace knowing that there won't be any war with China in the immediate future.

Prediction #17
How Pluto Will Impact Some Organisations

In 2017, the insurance company I was working for was under the threat of being taken over by a prominent bank.

'What do you think will happen to the company?' the CEO asked me.

'Nothing. Despite all the turmoil, the company will manage to stay afloat and survive all the odds. Its core identity will remain the same at least till 2020.'

I was confident since I knew the birth details of the organisation. I had joined the organisation in 2008 only after

---

[56] 'Uri Avenged: 35–40 Terrorists, 9 Pakistani Soldiers Killed in Indian Surgical Strikes, Say TV Reports', *Financial Express*, 29 September 2016, http://www.financialexpress.com/india-news/uri-avenged-35-40-terrorists-9-pakistani-soldiers-killed-in-indian-surgical-strikes-say-tv-reports/397625/.

looking at its birth chart. I wanted to see if I could stay there for a decade, and also if this would be the last corporate job before I quit working as a full-time employee. Both things happened as I expected.

Just like countries, organisations too have horoscopes. A horoscope drawn on the basis of the date and time of the establishment of the company reveals telling details about its future. Infosys was established on 7 July 1981, on the same day when M.S. Dhoni was born, and that was certainly not the only coincidence. Both had an impressive rise. Infosys went public in 1992, which was a remarkable year with Neptune and Pluto in super-strong positions.

Apple Inc. was founded on 1 April 1976. This was an excellent date with all the four centaurs—Planet-X, Planet-Y, Planet-Z and Chiron—either in exaltation or in their own house. Though this was a good date, the day the company went public, in 1980, was even more spectacular.

Some important dates add more significance to the journey of an organisation. It is always prudent to use both the establishment date and the 'going public' date for calculations, as more data usually gives better clarity. Sometimes a company changes shape, alters its identity, or is taken over by some other. All these dates, too, provide a lot of information about its potential and performance.

Reliance Commercial Corporation was founded in 1965—a great year, when the three superstar Khans of the Indian film industry were born. It was renamed as Reliance Industries Limited in May 1973, around the time when Sachin Tendulkar was born. It split into two factions in 2005, one of the most important years of the century, as there were seven higher hierarchy planets in the strongest positions that year. All this added to the strength of the company.

Within an organisation, the year when a brand is launched indicates even more specific milestones that it will reach, and also how it will do. Fair & Lovely, the fairness cream from Hindustan Unilever, was launched in 1975. The year was good and the brand did extremely well. But, due to backlash and criticism on promoting colourism, the company changed the brand name to Glow & Lovely in 2020.[57] The year 2020 was a milestone year, astrologically, and the re-naming of the brand took place at a good time, knowingly or unknowingly, and the product will continue to do very well under the new brand name.

The company itself changed its name from Hindustan Lever to Hindustan Unilever in 2007, a very good year. Its merger with Glaxo SmithKline Consumer Healthcare in 2020 throws up another positive astrological milestone.

Similarly, the transit of planets also indicates a favourable time period in the life cycle of an organisation. If a company has a weak Uranus during the time of establishment or incorporation, it will not do well during strong Uranus transits. If it was established during Pluto's Grey Lizard phase, it may hit a new low when Pluto transits a Grey Lizard patch.

Let us look at how some popular organisations will do in the years 2021–2040.

For the sake of simplicity, I have divided organisations on the basis of the year of establishment and given a blanket prognosis. We need to remember that this is a complex theory made simple and shouldn't be applied as it is. The list is small due to space constraints. The significant years on which the research—should I call it as equity research—was based are mentioned against the company.

Google and Alphabet (1998/2005/2015): When Google was founded, Pluto was in its own house. It has many brands, either acquired or unveiled during some extraordinary times, like Gmail in 2004 and YouTube in 2005. Google's date of

---

57   Rupam Jain, Charlotte Greenfield and Siddharth Cavale, 'Unilever's "Fair & Lovely" to get makeover after backlash,' *Reuters*, 25 June 2020, https://www.reuters.com/article/us-unilever-whitening-southasia-idUSKBN23W0W9.

reincorporation in 2002, and the initial public-offering date in 2004, are extraordinary times that made the company one of the biggest in the world.

However, at the same time, some very large hitches are seen in the incorporation dates of Google and Alphabet, the new entity that was created when Google was restructured in October 2015. The weak positions of Neptune and Saturn indicate some serious problems, and the Venus–Mars conjunction indicates some big legal troubles as well.

Though Alphabet was created long after Google was born, still Alphabet would now be treated as the parent company. October 2015 is a weak date with two major bodies, Uranus and Pluto, in debilitation. While the independent entities, and the brands under Google, are strong enough to grow and do well independently, Alphabet and Google as a group will have to deal with lots of issues.

HSBC: It was first established in 1865, first incorporated in 1866 and morphed into its current entity in 1991 as HSBC Holdings plc. What is amazing to note is that in all these three years Planet-X was in 'fall'. Planet-X goes into fall once in about sixty-three years and HSBC has restructured itself every time during the 'wrong' years. The planet responsible for money and finance is in the lowest position in the birth chart of a bank! No wonder HSBC has seen a deluge of scandals during its long history. Don't be surprised if the bank worth trillions of dollars, which has already been accused of allegedly doing transactions with terrorist organisations,[58] hits newer lows and courts even bigger scandals in the future. The bank would face some huge challenges and reach the brink of hara-kiri during the mid 2030s and early to mid-2040s when Planet-X will go into debilitation.

Hindustan Lever—1931/1933/1956/2007/2020: The organisation has had the best restructuring every time with its

---

[58] https://www.rollingstone.com/politics/politics-news/gangster-bankers-too-big-to-jail-102004/.

mergers and acquisitions, amongst all the Indian companies I have studied. Pluto, Uranus and Neptune, the top three planets, stand out during every milestone. The FMCG (fast moving consumer goods) giant will continue to grow by leaps and bounds during the next twenty years.

HDFC Bank: It was established in 1994. There are many weak planets in its chart—Jupiter, Saturn, Planet-Y, Planet-Z and Chiron. But what props up this bank is the sublime placement of the top three planets for monetary success and endurance— Pluto, Neptune and Planet-X. HDFC is already the largest private bank in the country. Expect this bank to beat all odds and keep growing in stature and success over the next two decades. A definite horse to bet on.

Here is a general classification of organisations into four types, on the basis of their incorporation and other major dates connected to their listing, acquisition, merger or reorganisation. If just the incorporation dates tell the story, I haven't added the other years. These companies are a part of the top organisations in India.[59] I have forecasted their performance over the next two decades. Please do note that any future mergers, reorganisation, restructuring and so on of the companies could alter the predictions.

Organisations that will do very well despite all odds—top four planets in strong positions:

1. Infosys—1981/1993
2. GlaxoSmithkline Pharmaceuticals—1924/1950
3. Hindustan Unilever—1931/1956/2007/2020
4. Maruti Suzuki—1981
5. State Bank of India—1955
6. Tata Consultancy Services—1968
7. Tata Motors—1945/1954/1991/2004
8. ICICI Bank—1994

---

[59] 'ET 500: 2020 Rankings', *The Economic Times*, 10 March 2021, https://economictimes.indiatimes.com/et500.

9. SAIL—1954
10. Reliance Industries—1964/1973/2005

Organisations that will slowly start declining or will go through some major crises unless something is done about them—strong planets with a mix of very weak planets; can be turned around with positive transformation:

1. Dr Reddy's Laboratories—1984
2. IDFC First Bank—2015/2016
3. Hero Motocorp—1984/2011
4. Kotak Mahindra Bank—1985/2003
5. Titan Company—1984/1993/2013
6. Bajaj Electricals—1938
7. ACC Limited—1936/2006
8. UCO Bank—1943
9. Grasim Industries Limited—1947
10. Zee Entertainment Enterprises—1982/1991/2006

Organisations that will face some grave problems/controversies/legal wrangles/drop in market share and may even shut down or be taken over:

1. Adani Group—1988/1993/2016
2. Piramal Enterprises Limited—1947/1984
3. Dabur—1884/2003/2012
4. Blue Star—1943
5. Jindal SAW Ltd—1984
6. Welspun India Ltd—1985
7. PNB Housing Finance—1988
8. Bajaj Finserv—2008
9. RBL Bank—1943/2010
10. Bombay Dyeing—1879

Some top companies that need to reinvent themselves, or they could start lagging behind new companies or could become large liabilities:

1. Biocon—1978
2. HDFC—1977
3. Indian Oil Corporation—1959
4. Larson & Toubro—1938
5. Mahindra & Mahindra—1945
6. Hindalco Industries—1958
7. GAIL India—1984
8. Ultratech Cement—1983
9. Sun Pharmaceuticals—1983
10. Bharti Airtel—1995

In general, expect organisations whose history started around 1937–1947, 1958–1961, 1983–1988 or 2007–2016 to face some trouble. If these organisations have already been taken over, and have had some major restructuring around strategic years, then they would manage to survive.

Expect organisations established around 1949–1956, 1963–1972, 1990–1994, 1997–2005 or 2019–2022 to do really well. Even organisations that were established in other years, but restructured during these years, will do reasonably well.

Prediction #18
Just Before Pluto Transits into Aquarius in 2038

In 1990, when Pluto just entered Scorpio, the internet was created. In 2020, when Pluto just entered Capricorn, the disruptive Covid-19 materialised. Both are events that changed the way the world would function. I'm very excited to try to know what will happen just before the dawn of the era of Pluto in Aquarius, around 2037–2038.

Capricorn is a traditional zodiac sign. During the entire period when Pluto is in Capricorn, between 2020 and 2038, the world would see the powers that be revert to ancient beliefs, practices and forms of governance. It is ironical that we are talking about the future where everything should be futuristic and forward-thinking should be the rule. However, as you go into the future, you realise that many industry practices and life in general would have remained old-school. How is that possible?

Let me try and explain how this dichotomy is possible. It started with Covid-19. When you look back at 2020, you see that all of a sudden everyone was locked up in their homes, doing basic stuff like cooking and dishwashing. Despite having all modern amenities at our fingertips, we still had to operate at very basic levels. This is one example of the impact of Pluto in the conservative Capricorn.

Let's look at a couple of things, and see how they are conservative when they could have been modern. In 2020, because of a virus, the entire industry had to undergo a transition. In most places, the workforce was cut down, and people working from home became the norm. But what you need to realise is that what we call as the 'new normal' is still at its infancy stage, and will require several more transitions before it becomes something innovative and extraordinary. The workplace has changed, but it is still traditional. This is just the starting point of a transition of how work will be performed in the future. Perhaps when Pluto enters Aquarius, the complete transformation will occur.

The virus, in its wake, will also not allow any optimism during 2021–2022. During the patch of Grey Lizard in 2025–2029, Capricorn, at its worst, can go through dark mood swings, depression, and can even become self-centred. The world will become much more materialistic and self-obsessed in this entire period of Pluto's stay in Capricorn. 'My' family, 'my' life, 'my' career will be the theme of this period.

Capricorn will also make this period very personality-oriented, with power being concentrated in certain pockets and with certain people. An invisible chain will bind people, media, economy and a general conservativism will be on the background in everything we do. Narrow vision based on the ideology of religion or other region-specific agendas would have flourished.

The later part of Pluto and Uranus at the peak of their exaltation in the 2030s will be a happy period. This period will be like the Capricorn reverse-age syndrome, where Capricorns behave like teens when they hit their fifties. But there is still a tinge of seriousness, practicality and responsibility associated with this period. Pluto will behave like a stern, old-school father.

Fast-forward to 2037–2038. Pluto would have pushed everything to its maximum potential and the markets, businesses and everything else would be at their peak. Some industries would have maxed out their potential, and they would not be able to grow beyond that. As all economists will tell you, after a peak there is a fall. Somewhere around 2037, if not slightly earlier, economic growth will start reversing.

During 2037–2039, expect some huge crashes in the stock market. Expect some big bubbles to burst. Some industries will fail, some big organisations will collapse, some governments will fall, before Pluto goes for another round of transformation and a fresh reset.

Pluto will be in 'father' avatar in Capricorn from 2020–2037. When Pluto enters Aquarius, it will be time to let loose and become a real teenager.

Pluto bought Covid in 2019 to make us stay at home and be with our families. Pluto will bring in something else in 2037–2038, something that we cannot envisage at this point of time, but something that will change our lives forever. Something that will break our souls free, something that will give us greater independence, something that will break all norms and something that will make us all equals in a positive way. Just as Covid bought pain initially before doing the reset, the happenings during 2037–2038, too, would be painful initially before setting us on the path to camaraderie, friendships, alliances and *esprit de corps* for the larger benefit of the society.

Prediction #19
Pluto in Aquarius (2039–2064) Era of Technical Blizzard
Pluto in exaltation
Eagle patch: 2039–2041
Grey Lizard patch: 2046–2049
Scorpion patch: 2057–2063

Many astrologers talk about the different 'ages'. They feel that a particular era—the number of years it lasts varies from theory to theory—would mould the behaviour of humans depending upon the zodiac sign. The zodiac sign of Aquarius is all about brotherhood, being friendly, living in peace and harmony. Well-known astrologers like Linda Goodman talk about an age lasting for even 2,000 years.[60] Linda feels the Aquarian age will dawn in 2150. I differ. I believe that the cycle of change doesn't come so late. It comes as frequent as once in 250 years.

I have a very simple understanding of the whole thing. The Aquarian age will start when Pluto will move into Aquarius. The planet of transformation, disruption and reset moving into the zodiac sign of innovation and technology—wow! This could be the most extraordinary twenty-five years, the precursor of sorts for the next 250 years.

Before we talk about the human aspects of Aquarius, let's talk about something else that Aquarians love—change! Aquarians love to do different things or do things differently. This era would all be about that. Take, for example, transport. Every mode of transport would have been extraordinarily changed. Speed of travel would have increased. Everything that Elon Musk stands for and thinks of, all the outlandish ideas, have

---

[60] 'Part 1//The Ages—The Age of Aquarius', *Linda-Goodman*, 6 September 2014, http://www.linda-goodman.com/ubb/Forum30/HTML/000127.html.

greater scope of happening during this period. Colonisation of Mars—if at all there is any scope for that—can only happen during this period. Renewable energy would be a norm. Musk would be considered a visionary because everything that he had envisaged of would happen then. There would be some people born during the early 2000s who would be driving this period— some visionaries who will change the world and the way we live.

This would be the era of real technology. Technology which we cannot even visualise or imagine now. There is going to be a blizzard of sorts in technology. Wearable technology? Yes. Every human being would be a number and be identified with some code. The whole world would be in sync. The only problem would be in distinguishing humans from the robots. Energy resources would have altered extraordinarily. Don't be surprised if your thought can make a machine work.

Human life expectancy would go up dramatically. Life would be extended as there would be an explosion of ways by which human body parts could be replaced. Bionic arms, brains with chips, artificial hearts—it won't be just about the knees as it is now. Living beyond a hundred would be commonplace. Every worn-out body part of yours could be replaced to stretch your life a little longer. How many ridiculous things can you think now? Aquarius is the most futuristic of all zodiac sign and all Aquarians reading this chapter, whatever you can envisage right now, even the most ridiculous, mind-bending innovations, will actually happen or start to take shape during this Aquarian age.

Marriage between humans and machine can happen. Probably marriage as an institution would become obsolete. You wouldn't need to meet a human being to make physical love any more. Kids would be surprised to know that there was a time when people used to live and love just one person. Well, talking about love, love would be in its purest form during this time of Aquarius. Loving another human being because he or she is a human being—not for the sake of their gender, colour, creed, religion or some other form of identity. If you think you are tolerant and liberal, think again. There is still a long way to go in terms of liberal thinking and this will be the period which will set things in that direction.

The Aquarian age would be one where the human being is spiritually evolved and probably the dawning of the age of the Aquarius would bring in more fellowship amongst human beings. We will see a collective conscience against the use of arms and terrorism will go down. There would be enhanced peace and camaraderie amongst people.

Aquarius is also about freedom. Along with freedom of expression, freedom of choosing life to live as you wish and freedom to do whatever you want will also happen during this time. In some parts of the world, there is still some repression due to religion, region, gender and other inequalities. Expect wars of different types to break out on these inequalities, so that the Aquarian spirit is set free.

Prediction #20

Can World War III Happen? When and why??

Every zodiac sign has some habits and characteristics associated with it that people from other zodiac signs find annoying. These would be the darkest negative traits of a particular zodiac sign. These traits could offer us clues about the reasons that could lead us to the next world war.

When will the next world war happen? Well, that should be the easier question to answer. During a Grey Lizard patch, for sure, especially if the Grey Lizard patch is followed by a few more years when at least two of the planets highest in the hierarchy, Uranus and Neptune, are also in weaker positions, along with Planet-X.

World War I started on 28 July 1914 and lasted till 11 November 1918. On the day it started, Pluto was in the Grey Lizard patch at

8'48" degrees in the zodiac sign of Gemini. Throughout this World War, Pluto remained in the Grey Lizard patch.

World War II started on 1 September 1939 and lasted till 2 September 1945. On the date it started, Pluto was in the Grey Lizard patch at 9'04" degrees in the zodiac sign of Cancer. Throughout World War II, Pluto stayed in the Grey Lizard patch. By the time it ended, all the three major planets, Uranus, Neptune and Pluto, were in debilitation.

The next world war can also happen only during a Grey Lizard patch. If World War III can be averted somehow during these four or five years of the Grey Lizard patch, we can be sure that any such possibility will only appear in the next patch—another twenty to thirty years away.

Now, let's come to the reasons why a world war happens. This is where it gets frightening, yet interesting. A world war happens when the zodiac signs draw out the worst feelings and emotions in people. Pluto is the culprit that catalyses them, and it does so during a Grey Lizard patch of a particular sign.

Let's look at the reasons why the first two world wars happened.

World War I happened because of great confusion. I have already quoted the German historian, Gerhard Hirschfeld, earlier on this subject. If you look at the series of events that led to the War, it is fascinating to note how this entire set of events would have been comic, not tragic, if only there had been better communication amongst the people involved. Geminians are master communicators. Their biggest vice is miscommunication. As mentioned earlier, a major breakdown in communication led to World War I.

Why did World War II happen? World War II was the goriest event ever witnessed by humans. Home, food, family, land and motherland are the biggest treasures for a Cancerian. The biggest trauma of their life would be to lose their home, their land, properties, and being killed because they belong to a particular section of the society. These gruesome sets of events happened because Pluto reached the Grey Lizard patch of Cancer and triggered them.

Let us now look at the next hundred years for the possible time and reasons for World War III. Needless to say, these will be Grey Lizard years.

Pluto in Capricorn—2025–2028: Quest for supremacy and wanting to enlarge one's territory. Greed and hunger for power of a leader. Smart manipulations and power struggles leading to the acquisition of new territories.

This is the patch which is of immediate importance to us. We need to check the horoscopes of major leaders for the possibility of an event of such huge magnitude. Leaders of nations who participate in a war are directly or indirectly responsible for killing of millions and that would reflect in their eighth house. The eighth house stands both for war and deaths. The eighth house would have planets in fall or debilitation of a leader who would be involved in bloody wars.

Let us examine the birth charts of a few prominent leaders of World War II. The leaders of the main Allies—Franklin D. Roosevelt and Winston Churchill—had strong debilitated planets in the eighth house. Winston Churchill the British prime minister, had a debilitated Neptune; Franklin Roosevelt, the American president, had a debilitated Saturn and Neptune. The birth details of the other main leader, Joseph Stalin, are not known. Amongst the main Axis leaders, Hirohito, emperor of Japan, had a debilitated Neptune in the eighth house; Adolf Hitler, dictator of Germany, had Pluto in fall in the eighth house and Benito Mussolini, prime minister of Italy, had Pluto in fall and Chiron in debilitation in the eighth house.

In case of a world war in 2025–2028, the horoscope of the major leaders at that time would become important and the examination of their eighth houses would reveal a possibility of such a major calamity. Let us examine if major planets are debilitated or in fall in the eighth house of the current important leaders:

Joe Biden, president of USA: None

Xi Jinping, president of China: Time of birth not known

Vladimir Putin, president of Russia: None

Narendra Modi, prime minister of India: None

Jair Bolsonaro, president of Brazil: None

Angela Merkel, chancellor of Germany: Jupiter in fall, insignificant

Kim Jong-un, supreme leader of North Korea: Time of birth not known

As we can see, the horoscope of current leaders of the largest nations do not show major bloodshed in their horoscopes. Even if the Chinese and the Korean leaders get into a war, there wouldn't be any supporters from any major country in the mayhem. It's highly unlikely that these set of leaders will be involved in a world war. Hence, I would say that there are little or no chances for a world war happening during the upcoming Grey Lizard patch of 2025–2028.

The assumption here is that the current leaders remain in their positions. If the heads of state during 2025–2028 are to be Grey Lizards born during 1958–1961 or if all or most of them have debilitated planets in the eighth house, then a World War III cannot be ruled out. But again, that looks least likely as even if a couple of the present leaders remain in their positions until then or are mentors to upcoming leaders, the major calamity can be averted. In India, the key second-rung leadership of BJP and the Congress doesn't have major debilitated planets in their eighth houses. At least from India's perspective, we can say that there would be no world war.

Pluto in Aquarius—2046–2049: A huge rebellion, leading to a chain of events that may cause a world war, is a possibility.

The war will probably be fought with ultra-sophisticated weapons during this high-tech era. These could be wars for liberating people rather than confining them. Destruction of the magnitude of WWI and WWII looks less likely though. Aquarius is a zodiac sign that believes in peace and brotherhood, and a war would pose as a disruption in peace. Such a war during Pluto in Aquarius could be averted by a group of peace-loving and friendly Aquarian leaders.

Pluto in Pisces—2071–2076: Pisces is about peace, spirituality, acceptance and wisdom. The opposite would be war, religious hatred, intolerance, bigotry, xenophobia and utter foolishness. I really doubt there could be a world war during the peaceful Pisces times but, if it does happen, these could be the reasons.

Pluto in Aries—2101–2106: Aries is the most virulent, violent, aggressive, controlling and dominating amongst all the zodiac signs. It makes me shudder to think what all could go wrong when Pluto enters a Grey Lizard patch during these times. All these vices would be at their worst, and could lead to one of the deadliest series of wars the world has ever seen. Uranus will also be in exaltation in Aries during this time, indicating that the weapons used for destruction will be the most advanced. Neptune will be in fall, and Planet-X too will go into deep debilitation soon after. If World War III has to happen, with all its deadliest aftermath, this seems to be the most likely time.

Prediction #21

The Next Big Recession (2045–2049)

Pluto in Grey Lizard in Aquarius
Neptune in debilitation in Aries
Uranus in fall in Leo

Planet-X in debilitation in Leo
2054–2056
Planet-X in fall in Scorpio

This is one prediction I do not want to live to see, but it seems it will happen within my lifetime. Having worked in the financial services industry, this prediction has been in the making for more than a couple of decades. After the last big recession in 2008–2009, my study has been deeper and much more detailed.

Many theories help to predict economic cycles. One simple thing to understand is that when you've hit the rock bottom, then the graph will only go up, and vice versa. But the biggest dilemma is how to know when you've hit the rock bottom—or the peak, either.

When you study the economic cycles, all the biggest dips in the markets have happened when at least two of the top four planets—Uranus, Neptune, Pluto and Planet-X—have reached the weakest of positions. Be it during the Tulip Mania of 1637, the Black Tuesday of 1929 or the recession of 2008, this was the common factor. Tulip Mania started when Neptune was slowly moving towards its deepest exaltation. Neptune is a planet of maya or mirage. It creates an artificial inflation of assets or an exaggeration in the markets. The prices of tulips remained high as long as Neptune was exalted. Just when it started getting debilitated, the markets crashed and the mania, created by Neptune, suddenly collapsed. It was like an artificial bubble that had burst. Neptune creates such bubbles.

During the Black Tuesday of 1929, markets crashed when Planet-X reached its fall position in Scorpio. In addition to Planet-X, Uranus was also in debilitation during this time. Planet-X comes in fall once every sixty-four years. Every time Planet-X comes into this position, there is some sort of a scam or scandal in the financial domain somewhere in the world.

Exactly after sixty-four years from 1929, in 1993, the Harshad Mehta scam happened in India.

Planet-X will cause a similar turbulence in the financial arena and some life-lessons will be learnt by human beings. Some scandal will rock the world and, in the aftermath, changes will be brought into the system, and new controls and regulations will be introduced to ensure that such a thing doesn't happen again. This is what happened in 1929, 1993 and will repeat itself between 2054 and 2056. The scam will be really massive and impact the entire world.

Something even bigger will happen when planets bigger than Planet-X are involved. The more important the planet, the bigger the crash. In 2008, both the top planets in the hierarchy—Neptune and Pluto—simultaneously got into deep debilitation. This comes once in about 200 years.

But a bigger crash awaits us.

Will such a huge crash happen again?

During 2047–2049, Pluto will be in the Grey Lizard avatar in Aquarius, Neptune will be in deep debilitation in Aries, Uranus will be in fall in Leo and Planet-X will be in debilitation in Leo. Additionally, even Chiron and Planet-Z will be debilitated. This is a very scary situation. All the top four planets will be in weak positions. This can only signal unprecedented torment for the world, the enormity of which we cannot imagine right now.

What could that be? During the first few years when Pluto enters Aquarius, around 2038–2040, there should be massive growth, and technological innovations would propel the world ahead. At this point of time, when Pluto goes into Grey Lizard, the grey shades of technological innovation will start showing up. The planetary positions point to a serious war-like situation and its whole destructive aftermath.

Since Pluto will be in the friendly Aquarius, I don't expect an actual war, but probably a technological war, or huge technological problems which may lead to some sort of a war somewhere. It cannot be exactly envisaged at this point of time. Only one thing is certain—it will wipe out gazillions from the market. Its magnitude may shake up the whole world. This will probably be the biggest crash between 2000 and 2050. And it will certainly be bigger than the 2008 market crash.

Thankfully for the world, 2050–2054 will be the time when Uranus once again gets exalted in the meticulous Virgo. All the financial transactions will undergo severe scrutiny and realignment. The financial domain itself will undergo massive transformation, after which life will go forward.

The 1929 crash was followed by Pluto's debilitation, resulting in the Depression, in the 1930s. Once the 2055–2057 period is sorted out, Pluto, still exalted, will move towards the peaceful Pisces, and then there will be prosperity for a long period once again.

Prediction #22

The Importance of Being Kamala Harris

'It is going to be Joe Biden,' I declared.

I had been invited by Reuters as one of the experts to predict the outcome of the 2020 US presidential elections in the Global Markets Forum, an online meeting, held on 2 November 2020. When I said this, the correspondent from Reuters was amused. 'I'm surprised,' she said. 'Our analysis and numbers show the clear winner in Donald Trump.' Well, it seems, in their analysis, they clearly left out one very important component of the Democratic party's bid to win the election—Kamala Harris.

Kamala has an exceptional horoscope. She was born on a full-moon day. She also has Chiron, Neptune and Pluto in the deepest exaltation. This is similar to Shah Rukh Khan or Jeff Bezos. She has the same set of planets, but moulded for politics. Joe Biden has Planet-X in the deepest exaltation. At that time, it was transiting his seventh house of winning over enemies in politics, and hence I could predict with confidence, on a YouTube video, uploaded on 1 October 2020, that Joe Biden would become the forty-sixth president of the United States. [61]

There was another reason why I said that Joe Biden would be the next president. A closer look at the horoscopes of Kamala Harris and Joe Biden showed certain interesting events in the coming months.

The extraordinary placement of Planet-X has pushed Biden to the highest position in the country. Planet-Y, his eleventh lord, will also get exalted in 2021, in his first house, fulfilling the original promise in his horoscope—that he would occupy the highest position in the latter part of his life. So far so good.

All the top three planets—Uranus, Neptune and Pluto—were in debilitation in the birth chart of Joe Biden. The most important planet, Pluto, is currently transiting his third house since 2020. The third house indicates the mind, the tongue and movement. There have been many observations that Biden faces impediments while communicating.[62] There were comments during the elections and at the time of his election speeches. He has already showed some of these signs, like coughing and spluttering, and he also hurt his leg while playing with his dog. When Pluto moves into a strong position, Biden's condition will only get worse. His mind, his tongue and probably the legs could be severely afflicted. He could also face restrictions in his movements.

Uranus is currently exalted, but was debilitated in his birth chart and hence is a conflicting force. Right now it is in his

---

[61]   Greenstone Lobo, 'Donald Trump or Joe Biden?' *YouTube*, 1 October 2020, https://www.youtube.com/watch?v=jz-vWTeVmcc&t=4s.

[62]   Svar Nanan-Sen, 'Joe Biden Health Fears: President-Elect Coughs Non-Stop in Speech "You're scaring us!" ', *Express*, 15 December 2020, https://www.express.co.uk/news/world/1372687/joe-biden-health-fears-coughing-speech-us-election-2020-electoral-college-latest-vn.

sixth house. The sixth house indicates health, and having a weak transit to the house doesn't really augur well for the president's health. He is America's oldest elected president ever, and may not be physically and mentally at his hundred per cent. Besides, a weak Neptune will transit into his fifth house, which represents government work, in 2022, clearly indicating that he wouldn't be in a position to do his high-level government and diplomatic work for too long.

Now, let us look at the horoscope of Kamala Harris. While the power of Planet-X and Planet-Y was pushing Biden to become the president, Kamala's horoscope was waiting for some interesting events to unfold. Kamala's sixth lord, Pluto, is transiting her eighth house. And her tenth lord, Neptune, is the most important planet of her horoscope, and will enter its own house in 2022. The eighth house indicates some transformation, some huge changes and obstacles. Thus Kamala's horoscope indicates that there will be some unforeseen, transformational events that may catapult her into the position of the highest authority.

This could mean multiple things. Maybe Biden's health would not permit him to perform the daily chores of the president. Kamala may become a shadow president, while Biden is still the nominal president, constitutionally. Planet-X is still in her twelfth house of working behind the scenes, so this scenario could be a possibility.

It could mean even bigger and stranger things. Planet-X will move into Kamala's first house of personality in 2022. With Neptune already strongly placed in her tenth house of career, it could accord her a greater control over larger spheres of the administration. Kamala is going to be powerful for sure—very powerful. For all we know, she may go on to be a president, duly elected. Or her fate may have something else in store, even before the next elections. Whatever happens, the next four years of Biden's presidency promise to be interesting.

Prediction #23

India under Narendra Modi until 2024

Since 2009, when I made my first politics forecast, I have correctly predicted the outcome of the general elections in India. Predicting the outcome of the elections in 2019 was a relatively easy task.[63] I just had to figure out if anyone had a stronger horoscope than Narendra Modi. The Bharatiya Janata Party had played it smart by making it a personality-based election for the second consecutive term. In 2014, they rode on the Modi wave and, in 2019, it was Modi wave-2.

Narendra Modi was born in 1950, when Pluto was in nascent exaltation in his eleventh house, indicating that he would become even more successful and keep growing in stature as he grew older. Exactly seventy years later, in 2019, Pluto was getting exalted once again, and it was bound to favour him. The transiting Uranus, getting exalted in his seventh house, helped him further by vanquishing his known political enemies.

How will Modi's government shape up in the remaining term?

The horoscope of the leader of the nation also indicates what is going to happen in the country. In late 2019, during transit, Pluto, Modi's second lord, moved into his fourth house. For Modi, it was about the second lord, of wealth, transiting into the fourth house of the motherland. Before Covid appeared, I believed that after getting a consecutive term, Modi would focus on measures to enhance wealth-creation and development of business in the country. The globetrotting prime minister, in his second term, would focus on the nation by staying put in his country. Only after Covid struck did it become clear that Modi would be, in a way, forced to focus on the aspects of the fourth house of his horoscope—his motherland. Reforms like development of smart cities or infrastructural developments

---

[63] Greenstone Lobo, 'Who Will Be India's Prime Minister in 2019?', *YouTube*, 6 March 2019, https://www.youtube.com/watch?v=XslJsb5FYS0&t=46s.

may have always been a part of the plans of the government, but Covid would have given them a clearer direction. With the country facing droughts, floods, employment and many other 'local' challenges, the Prime Minister's focus would be on solving the problems of the sons of the soil, right from farmers to students or business people. As I mentioned earlier, astrology can point out the areas where the action will be, but we don't always know exactly what it will be until it happens.

Narendra Modi also has Neptune transiting into his sixth house of health. He has a weak Neptune in his birth chart and this is an opposing force. Earlier when analysing his horoscope, I used to think that he would face some personal health challenges. Now it is clear that it is the health problems of his country that he will have to tackle during his governance. Also, as the planet is negatively placed, the Oxygen (Neptune again) supply issue came to the fore.

The appointment of two other people in important positions also baffled me initially—that of Nirmala Sitharaman, a 1959-born Grey Lizard, as the finance minister of the country; and Uddhav Thackeray, another 1960-born Grey Lizard, as the chief minister of Maharashtra. I decided to wait and observe. Grey Lizards face the biggest tasks and struggles to script some extraordinary turnaround stories. Barack Obama, a Grey Lizard, became the president of America when the USA was going through its worst economic crisis. Uddhav Thackeray became the chief minister of Maharashtra, when Maharashtra was facing its biggest crisis in Covid-19. Nirmala Sitharaman is tasked with the biggest responsibility of turning the country's economy around during its worst crisis.

Despite the country reeling under the impact of Covid and the sluggish growth of the economy, there are reasons to look forward to better times ahead in the remaining period of Modi's term. Planet-X will move into the ninth house of luck for Narendra Modi in May 2022 and will start the period of positive waves in India. Covid would have practically ended by then as both Neptune and Pluto would have moved out of their nascent positions. Planet-X transiting into Gemini will bring back the cheer in the markets and the movement and travel of people reviving 'normalcy' in life. The various activities required to pitchfork the economy will be set in motion.

The good news is that Modi's horoscope promises that he and his team will be able turn the economy of the country around from bad to good despite the ongoing Covid challenge. In the next four years India will stride forward in all spheres. This is reflected by the transit of Pluto, Modi's second lord, into his fourth house. The second house means wealth and business development, and the fourth house means motherland. The Make-in-India movement will gain momentum and create multitudes of new businesses. India will become a better and more attractive destination for foreign investors. The decision to privatise some of the government-owned banks is,[64] again, a positive fallout of the movement of Pluto, the second lord, as the second house also indicates the sector of finance.

Expect massive positive measures to be put in place to push the economy further. Pluto's placement in the fourth house indicates the huge infrastructure endeavours that will be taken up by the Modi government. Expect more high-tech cities built in free economic zones, railway corridors, rivers being connected, and golden quadrilaterals connecting different cities. The fourth house indicates housing. There could possibly be increase in efforts made for low-cost housing in India.

Talking about wealth creation, expect a huge bull run in these years and the Sensex to break new barriers. A 5-trillion-dollar economy by 2024? Possible, very possible. If

---

[64]   PTI, 'Privatisation of PSU Banks: Govt to Bring Amendments to Two Legislations', *Mint*, 16 February 2021, https://www.livemint.com/industry/banking/privatisation-of-psu-banks-govt-to-bring-amendments-to-two-legislations-11613463939073.html.

India doesn't reach there, it will be very close to it. Just the effort to accomplish it would produce a positive push in all areas of economy.

The Modi government faced a huge backlash[65] for the management of the Covid crisis. But by the end of his second term, Modi and his team would be able to showcase that his government had indeed done a good job during the crisis. And that will ensure a huge platform for a positive narrative for the next election.

Prediction #24

Russia under Vladimir Putin until 2024 and Beyond

Vladimir Putin has already been the president of Russia thrice. He has also been the prime minister of the country twice. He has the right to seek re-election in 2024. The main questions we have are—Will Putin be re-elected? If so, how will Russia do under his leadership over the next decade?

Planet-X in Taurus in the eighth house produces very strong leaders—leaders who storm their way to the top, crush opposition mercilessly, rule their nations with an iron fist, and stay in power for a long time. Experts feel that under the leadership of Putin, Russia has reversed its movement to democracy.[66] Human rights organisations and activists accuse him of persecuting political critics and activists, as well as of ordering them to be tortured or assassinated. Experts do not consider Russia a democracy, citing the jailing of political opponents, restricts press freedom, and the lack of free and fair elections[67]. Eighth house is all about authority and control,

---

65   https://www.theguardian.com/world/2021/may/17/everybody-is-angry-modi-under-fire-over-indias-covid-second-wave.

66   Larry Diamond, 'Facing Up to the Democratic Recession, *Journal of Democracy*, January 2015, https://www.journalofdemocracy.org/articles/facing-up-to-the-democratic-recession/.

67   Graeme Gill, *Building an Authoritarian Polity: Russia in Post-Soviet Times* (Cambridge University Press, 2015).

and Putin very clearly reflects the position of Planet-X in his eighth house.

Putin has Pluto in exaltation in the eleventh house in the second-half of his life, indicating that his control and dominance will continue. Pluto will remain exalted for more than a decade, and Putin's influence, too, will run till the end of the 2020s. Putin will certainly be re-elected in the 2024 presidential elections, and remain in power till 2030.

The biggest positive factor about a leader with dominant planets in the eighth house is that they ensure they do whatever they have set out to do, brushing away all the opposition forces. Putin has Pluto in exaltation, now traversing the fourth house of his motherland, very clearly indicating that Russia will continue to grow massively over the next decade. Falling oil prices and international sanctions post–2014, after Russia's annexation of Crimea, led to the Russian GDP shrinking by 3.75 per cent.[68] Putin's second term was not as successful, since Pluto was in debilitation during 2010–2020.

Right now, in 2021, Pluto is Putin's second lord and it is exalted. The second house indicates monetary benefits; exaltation in the fourth house indicates benefits for the country. Expect the Russian economy to grow dramatically during this decade. Russia forms a part of the elite BRICS (Brazil, Russia, India, China, South Africa) nations. Right now Russia ranks between eleven and twenty in the GDP rankings. By the time Putin hangs up his boots, he would have taken Russia into the top ten. There will be more jobs, a better economy, and a higher happiness quotient in the Russian population in the 2020s. Many years later, when the Vladimir Putin presidency is evaluated, he would be judged positively from a larger historical perspective despite the high-handed politics he is said to have practised.

---

[68] Shaun Walke and Alberto Nardelli, 'Russia's Rouble Crisis Poses Threat to Nine Countries Relying on Remittances', *The Guardian*, 18 January 2015, https://www.theguardian.com/world/2015/jan/18/russia-rouble-threat-nine-countries-remittances.

Prediction #25

Can Sonia Gandhi Bring Back the Magic of the Congress?

Whenever I make any political predictions in India, I clarify that whatever I'm predicting is purely on the basis of astrology, and that I do not have leftist, rightist, centrist views, or any sort of political affiliations, whatsoever. I reiterate that here.

Sonia Gandhi has a really interesting horoscope. She has her Planet-X in exaltation in her ninth house. That made her travel from one country, and live her entire life in another. Planet-X is so deeply exalted in her chart that it shows she will go on to become an extremely powerful person in a foreign country. Unfortunately for Sonia, Planet-X is the only positive planet in her horoscope. There is a strong Venus, which gave her strong love, and a relationship that took her to a country thousands of miles away from her birth place.

Sonia has her seventh lord, Saturn, in fall, which took away her husband at a young age. Besides, she also has a weak fourth house with Chiron in debilitation, which indicates that her children would go through huge adversities. The weakest planet of her horoscope is the fifth lord, Pluto, in debilitation. The fourth and the fifth houses co-rule children and the weak planets don't really augur well for the Gandhi family. This indicates that Sonia will face a lot of anxieties due to her children, and her biggest grief will be in that area.

During the period between 2020 and 2038, Pluto will be traversing her seventh house. The seventh house indicates politics and political enemies. Pluto is strong at this time, but debilitated in her birth chart, and that too moving into the seventh house now, spells bad news for Sonia Gandhi and the Congress Party. If her horoscope is any indication, then during the decade, from 2020 to 2030, the Congress Party will find it difficult to win elections and go on to form a government.

Sonia will only see a decline in her position in the public space as the seventh house represents public domain.

Pluto is her fifth lord (of children) and debilitated in the seventh house (of public success and acceptance). This position indicates that her children may face tribulations in the public domain, which could have several implications. One of the implications may be that Priyanka and Rahul will find it difficult to succeed in politics at the highest level.

Sonia also has a weak eighth Lord, Uranus, in the eleventh house in her birth chart. This could also mean that she may stay away from active politics due to failing health.

The matriarch's horoscope indicates that all is not well with the grand old party of India, and that it will continue to be so for some more time.

Prediction #26
Can Rahul or Priyanka Gandhi Be the Prime Minister?

Rahul and Priyanka were born in 1970 and 1972, respectively, with Uranus in deep exaltation. Rahul has it in 11 degrees and Priyanka in 24. Rahul has Uranus in the twelfth house and Priyanka in the fourth. The deeply exalted planet shows the kind of prominent people they are. Priyanka has the planet exalted in the fourth house of family, which indicates the pedigree she comes from. Rahul has it in the twelfth house of foreign countries or losses.

Rahul's horoscope clearly reflects the huge losses he had to face in some elections, while spearheading the Congress party. Even though Uranus is exalted, as Rahul doesn't have much to do with foreign countries, it has manifested into losses for him. Uranus, his fifth lord of fame, in the twelfth house of losses, indicates loss even in popularity due to certain gaffes he has made. I had predicted earlier in 2019, before, that Rahul Gandhi can't win against Narendra

Modi.[69] I had pointed this out due to the position of Uranus in his horoscope.

Rahul's decision to step down from the position of the president of the Congress party was probably right. Unfortunately, he doesn't have it in him to lead the party to a huge victory or to capture the Parliament, any time in the future. If at all he decides to make a comeback, it should only be after 2031. A person needs to have a very powerful planet in the fourth, fifth, seventh or tenth house in the birth chart or in transit, to have a chance for the highest position in a country.

And, even if you do have it, you need to have it better placed than your opponent. This is what happened with Rahul in 2019. Though he had Uranus transiting his seventh house, Narendra Modi, who has the same ascendant, also had Uranus transiting the same house, simultaneously. And because Modi had a better horoscope, he got the better of Rahul.

Rahul will have Uranus getting into exaltation again in 2031–2037, this time in the ninth house. Just like in 2019, as he is a member of parliament, he could still be one even in the 2030s. The Congress party will have better chances of bouncing back if they have a person born between the 1950s and the 1960s as a prime ministerial candidate for the next two elections—in 2024 and 2029.

Even after 2029, Rahul Gandhi should never be a prime ministerial candidate, as he can never become the prime minister. Like in 2019, projecting Rahul Gandhi as the PM would only harm the chances of Congress party even in the future.

Due to the placement of Uranus in his twelfth house of losses, it wouldn't be surprising if he decides to rid himself of all the troubles and stays away from politics altogether. That would be like an abdication of sorts, which is also an indication

69   Greenstone Lobo, 'Who Will Be India's Prime Minister in 2019?' *YouTube*, 7 March 2019, https://www.youtube.com/watch?v=XslJsb5FYS0&list=RDQMB-OhHWIhwpc&index=1.

of the twelfth house. The second probability, and a better path for Rahul would be to become the behind-the-scenes-power, who runs the show away from the limelight. That is also a positive manifestation of the twelfth house, Uranus.

Between the two, Priyanka Gandhi has a better horoscope that may take her to a high position in politics. The strong seventh house indicates that she could play a bigger role in politics later. Planet-Z will enter her third house in 2025. The third house points towards strategic leadership. This may be when she can assume a position of leadership or, if she already has, then she will be able to make some significant contributions.

But her highest elevation in life will come only after 2031, when Uranus gets exalted in her first house (personality). Will that highest elevation be the office of the prime minister? Well, that is a big question. Prima facie, her horoscope shows chances of being the leader of a party or occupying high offices in the government, but not necessarily that of the prime minister. It also boils down to who her opponent will be in the 2030s.

That means in the 2024 elections, if the Congress has to have any chances of winning, they need to field another senior person as a prime minister candidate, preferably someone born in the 1950s or 1960s. Otherwise, they will have to wait for another term, or maybe two. Between 2025 and 2030, when Uranus is debilitated, Rahul and Priyanka will go through extreme difficulties in politics, and also huge personal losses. They can turn their luck around in the 2030s if they play their cards well.

Prediction #27

Can Amit Shah Become the Prime Minister?

Amit Shah as PM, anyone?

The number two[70] most influential politician in the country

---

[70] Malini T., 'India's 10 Most Influential Politicians, 2020', *Yahoo!News*, 24 September 2020, https://in.news.yahoo.com/indias-10-most-influential-

when this book is being written in 2021, he definitely has a chance to become number one.

Amit Shah has Neptune, his seventh lord, exalted. The seventh house indicates politics, and a deeply exalted Neptune suggests the extent of influence he has on the political landscape of India. He also has his third lord Pluto in exaltation in the twelfth house. The third house indicates the mind, leadership and strategy, and the twelfth house indicates working behind the scenes.

These two houses bring out the gist of what Amit Shah is all about. He is the chief strategist for the BJP.[71] He has masterminded their strategies shrewdly to topple the opposition and ensure victory for his party, in the elections. Pluto's exaltation in the twelfth house adds to the fact that he remains in the background while discharging his duties. All the work he does visiting states, those plans and rallies, happens in the background before the grand results come up. His actions are manifestations of his Pluto in the background.

Amit Shah isn't done yet. While he has done all the legwork (again, the twelfth house) these years, he may rise to greater limelight in the future. Pluto, in transit in 2020, has moved into exaltation into his fifth house, and Neptune has moved into its own house, that is, the seventh house. That is phenomenal. Both the fifth and the seventh houses indicate the government. The seventh house specifically indicates influence over people and victory over enemies. This clearly shows that Amit Shah's influence on India's political landscape will keep growing in the future. He will play a very powerful role in the government, bigger than what he has played so far. Can he be the prime minister? The chances are very high.

---

politicians-2020-yahoo-india-090538883.html.

71   PTI, 'Amit Shah: BJP's "Chanakya" Who Delivered Modi Wave 2.0', *The Times of India*, 23 May 2019, https://timesofindia.indiatimes. com/india/amit-shah-bjps-chanakya-who-delivered-modi-wave-2-0/ articleshow/69465902.cms.

Is there anyone in the competition? If you look at the logical progression of the years when the planets were placed in very powerful positions after 1950 (the current PM of India, Narendra Modi, was born in 1950), it happened in the patch of 1964–1966. These were the years when the two most powerful planets in the universe, Pluto and Neptune, came into the deepest exaltation. India has to have a PM who was born in that patch. As of now, we can see no one else in the country, born during that time, so powerful and visible, so Amit Shah seems to be the chosen one.

The other powerful patch is 1953–1956. There are a few politicians born in this patch but Amit Shah's chances are higher. Since Pluto and Neptune stay in the fifth and the seventh house for a decade-and-a-half Amit Shah will be a force to reckon with for a long time to come.

There are many young and interesting national-level politicians in India. If we bracket them according to their age and planetary groups, those born in the 1970s will come to power only later. And amongst those born in the 1960s, no one has better planets than Amit Shah.

If you need to know what important role this current number two will play in the future, look at the current second-in-command of the United States. Kamala Harris, the vice president of the United States, was born just a couple of days apart from Amit Shah. And that, people, is not a coincidence. It shows the planetary strength of these two and also provides a hint on how things will unfold in the future. They both have horoscopes so similar that we can chart out one person's life looking at the course of the other.

Prediction #28
Can Arvind Kejriwal Have a National Impact?

Arvind Kejriwal caught the fancy of the common people. He gave India a third option, creating the Aam Aadmi Party (AAP).

It was a fresh alternative, which did not come with any baggage. It didn't belong to any extremes regarding political alignment, and generally looked progressive.

Arvind Kejriwal has an interesting horoscope. His seventh lord, Pluto, is exalted in the fourth house, indicating that he would be a strong political leader. His Uranus, is exalted in the fifth house and suggests that he would form a government. He has already been the chief minister of Delhi. What next? Can he take AAP to the national level? Well, that's where his horoscope falls short.

The snags in his horoscope are twofold here. First of all, his Pluto is exalted at 28 degrees and not deep enough. which is beyond the deepest exaltation point of 25 degrees. The deepest exaltation happened during 1964–1967. That means though Kejriwal has a horoscope strong enough to bring in a change, it wouldn't be a sweeping change in the country. Everyone who has ever changed the political landscape of a country—be it Mahatma Gandhi, Nelson Mandela, or a prime minister or a head of state like Manmohan Singh or Joe Biden—was born during a strong planet exalted in its nascent or deepest position.

People born around the deepest exaltation points will hover around the periphery. They end up as the second-bests in a country, or lead the states within the country, or remain confined to lesser roles. If Kejriwal faces a political opponent born during 1964–1967 at the national level, he, a 1968-born, wouldn't be able to beat him or her.

Kejriwal's challenging planets compound the issues here. He has Neptune in nascent debilitation in his seventh house of political enemies and leadership. It means that Kejriwal has enemies stronger than him, and he will find it difficult to overcome them many times. He would also be a slightly weak leader who would find it difficult to remain in control and keep his party motivated.

Also, consider the fact that he has a weak eleventh house. Neptune will transit this in the 2020s. The eleventh house indicates the later part of life, and Kejriwal would find the going difficult as the years pass by. He does have it in him to be a leader with a national voice, but he doesn't have it in his horoscope to be a dominant power to overcome all his political enemies and form a government at the centre. A state or two can be conquered, but forming a government at the centre can only be a distant dream.

Prediction #29
Can Yogi Adityanath Play a National Role?

It is fascinating that an ascetic has become a politician. He rules an Indian state and probably can even show significance at the national level.

Yogi Adityanath has a very powerful horoscope. How powerful? If I have to offer a comparison, I would compare his chart to the Canadian Prime Minister Justin Trudeau's. The strengths of both their horoscopes are similar and their important planets, connected to politics, are in the same positions. Yogi Adityanath's spiritual connection comes from Planet-Y in exaltation in his ninth house. The most powerful planets in his horoscope are Pluto and Uranus. Together they form a power centre. Uranus is his seventh lord and its exaltation, together with Pluto, the fourth lord of influence in the motherland, shows why he went beyond spirituality.

Yogi's best times will come in the 2030s, when his Uranus gets exalted in his eleventh house. The eleventh house stands for the later part of life. This means Yogi could be influential even in his fifties. Could this period be when he attains a position of national importance?

Highly possible!

After the 1964–1967 patch, the 1970–1972 patch assumes higher significance with respect to powerful political leaders. There could be a prime minister emerging from this patch. It is too early to say if Yogi can go on to be a prime minister as leaders in the opposition, who aren't visible right now, may emerge in the next few years as competition. But, looking at the strength of just his horoscope, we cannot rule out that possibility.

Let us examine the possible competitors to Yogi. Priyanka Gandhi will have her Uranus exalted in the first house in 2031– 2038, which means that there could be a personal elevation in her life. One hurdle for Priyanka is her fourth lord, and for Yogi, it is his seventh lord. The seventh lord symbolises being elected, and the fourth lord means being influential in your motherland. For a politician, the seventh house is a much better option—like Trudeau again. The associated political team that each leader has, is crucial to who forms a government. If Priyanka manages to groom a set of younger leaders and has a good team in place, it seems the elections in the 2030s will produce a really nail-biting finish.

Many more younger players will be visible in due course and may need to be considered in the forecasts. Some players in the fray, at this point, include Jyotiraditya Scindia, Sachin Pilot, Devendra Fadnavis and Akhilesh Yadav. Among them, only Sachin Pilot doesn't have a strong horoscope to make him a prime ministerial candidate, unlike the others.

It is safe to conclude that Yogi does have a great chance to achieve the highest office. But we will talk more about this in the future. It looks like the 2030s will be a very interesting time in Indian politics.

Prediction #30
The Prince Will Finally Be the King

Prince Charles has been the king-in-waiting for almost seventy-five years, as Queen Elizabeth II was not ready to abdicate the throne in favour of her not-so-young son. That she is nearly a century old is a different story altogether.

Many people in the United Kingdom have this romantic idea that if Prince Charles becomes the king, he should abdicate the throne and pass it voluntarily to Prince William.[72] The general feeling is that Prince William is at the right age to be the king and can perform the duties for a long time and more efficiently. But this romantic idea will not come true.

Pluto has already entered Prince Charles's seventh house of impact on people and elevation. For the Royals, this could translate into a coronation, even if it is only a formality. Pluto is in an exalted position after almost fifty-five years. Prince Charles had to wait for so long because of this reason, and he won't let that chance pass so easily.

He will be the king very soon because the ailing Queen may step down from her duties, or pass away. The wait will be over for Prince Charles and we will see some royal festivities in Buckingham Palace.

And yes, the wait for Prince William will become longer.

Prediction #31
Will Megxit Prove to Be a Right Move?

It all started when Prince Harry was born. The planets in his birth chart are in Leo and Aries. Leo stands for royalty, and Aries stands for 'me first'. Harry would have made a fantastic Royal had he been the first-born. He is sixth in the line of succession, which eliminates the possibility of becoming a king—ever. A Leo denied kingship is like a lion denied kingship of the jungle. Like Harry, Anil Ambani and Mukesh Ambani have strong Aries in their horoscopes, and each one wanted to be the number one. However, there can only be one person at the top. Anil moved out, so has Harry.

---

[72] Jenzia Burgos, 'Royal Followers Want Prince William to Be Their Next King After the Queen Steps Down', *SC*, 15 December, 2020, https://stylecaster.com/prince-william-king-queen-elizabeth/.

Yes, Prince Harry indeed hates the camera flash.[73] He says they remind him of his mother's death. But he doesn't allow that hatred for unwanted intrusion into his privacy to mask his need to be known for his individuality. An Aries wants to be the boss, and a Leo loves being a star, but in their own right and on their own terms. A Leo loves to 'give', not to receive. The scrutiny of his annual expenditure from the grants received from the taxpayers would have been a huge burden on the Leo Harry's heart.

On their Instagram post Harry and Meghan say, 'We intend to step back as "senior" members of the Royal Family and work to become financially independent, while continuing to fully support Her Majesty The Queen.'[74] The phrase 'financially independent' assumes importance here. Harry would love to make a fortune on his own and prove that he can be a 'king' in his own right.

Prince Harry and Meghan Markle are powerful influencers,[75] and have many ways to cash in on their popularity. They will certainly not hide from public glare, but will selectively control marketing themselves and their influencer status. They have shifted base to North America, opened up and are ready to sell parts of their lives to select media. They have started with Netflix[76] and the much-publicised Meghan Markel's interview

[73] Rebecca Speare-Cole, 'Prince Harry Says He's Reminded of His Mother Princess Diana's Death Every Time He Sees a Camera Flash', *Evening Standard*, 18 October 2019, https://www.insider.com/prince-harry-talks-about-princess-diana-death-africa-documentary-2019-10.

[74] The Duke and Duchess of Sussex (@sussexroyal), *Instagram*, 9 January 2020, https://www.instagram.com/p/B7EaGS_Jpb9/.

[75] Rachel Deeley and M.C. Nanda, 'Could Meghan Markle Cash In on Her Powerful Influencer Status?' *BoF*, 9 January 2020, https://www.businessoffashion.com/articles/media/could-meghan-markle-cash-in-on-her-powerful-influencer-status.

[76] Brooks Barnes, 'Prince Harry and Meghan Sign Megawatt Netflix Deal', *The New York Times*, 2 September 2020, https://www.nytimes.com/2020/09/02/business/media/harry-meghan-netflix.html.

with Oprah Winfrey[77]. They have announced plans to start an NGO though their other plans are not clear at this point. Will the couple find their financial independence and live happily ever after?

Planets show that this decision may prove to be wrong for the prince and his actress wife. Prince Harry has Pluto, his twelfth lord of foreign countries and losses, transiting into his second house of wealth. It will remain here for about eighteen years. With Pluto in debilitation in the second house, Prince Harry will find it challenging to create huge wealth independently. His business ideas, or the lack of them, would mean that he won't be able to create the great wealth he thought he would be able to on his own.

Pluto could lead to a long struggle with finances. Their lifestyle requires huge funds and the revenue they generate may fall short of their expectations and requirements. After a decade or so, the money he has inherited from his family will be the saviour, and not what he set out to acquire. Neptune indicates family possessions in the fourth house. It is the strongest planet in his chart, and not Pluto, which indicates wealth created by one's own effort.

Meghan's chart is a shade better than Prince Harry's in matters of finance. She should be able to do more on her work front and generate more income from her endeavours than him, which may not be a happy space for the Leo in Harry. A royal wanting to earn his own money by working hard is not an ego trip. It is sensible. All the royals should do it instead of living on taxpayers' money. But Prince Harry's weak horoscope will stop him from achieving his goal.

Overall, the move to leave the royal family will not meet its purpose of financial freedom.

Prince Harry has upset the applecart and will realise his mistake, though he may never admit to it. The continuous

---

[77] https://www.cbsnews.com/live-updates/oprah-winfrey-interviews-meghan-markle-prince-harry/

financial drain he faces over the next two decades will tell a different story, though.

Prediction #32
How Will Japan Fare under Emperor Naruhito?

Emperor Naruhito's father, Emperor Akihito, became the first Japanese emperor to abdicate the throne in more than 200 years. On 1 May 2019, when Crown Prince Naruhito ascended the Chrysanthemum Throne as the new emperor, Japan also welcomed a new era called 'Heisei', which means 'beautiful harmony'. What does Japan's new era look like for Emperor Naruhito?

The emperor in Japan has no political responsibilities and is largely a ceremonial figure. But the emperor's birth chart, despite the lack of any active role in running the country, still reflects the health of the country, and will help us understand what is in store for the island nation.

Emperor Naruhito is a Grey Lizard, born in 1960. As he doesn't have a son, his brother, Fumihito, will ascend the throne after him. The Grey Lizard has already done its job partially, as his lineage ends here.

The Emperor's Pluto will remain in his seventh house of public life till 2037, after which it will enter the eighth house of transition. Before this, there could be some movement, and Emperor Naruhito's time on the throne may be short-lived. As Pluto was in a Grey Lizard avatar when he was born, the Emperor will face serious obstacles in his life when the transiting Pluto reaches the Grey Lizard position in 2025.

There will also be some serious troubles for the country he rules. Japan's economic growth is currently stuck at one per cent,[78] while neighbouring countries like China and South

---

[78] Mohamed A El-Erian, 'Commentary: The Low-Growth Trap Japan Is Stuck in Is Spreading Across the World', *CNA*, 16 April 2019, https://www.channelnewsasia.com/news/commentary/low-growth-new-normal-ageing-population-trap-japan-strategies-11425590.

Korea are on a growth trajectory. Japan will get stuck in a rut during these four years from 2025 to 2028 of the Grey Lizard. During these four years, Japan will go through some particularly tough situations. The country is prone to natural calamities, and they could exacerbate an already bad situation during this phase. Some unusual events detrimental to the economy and the country's well-being, could also occur during this time.

Japan should avoid any kind of diplomatic disputes during this phase, as many circumstances could push it to the brink. We cannot anticipate all events as of now, but they could happen during this emperor's regime.

Prediction #33

Will Emmanuel Macron Be Re-elected?

The youngest French president ever, Emmanuel Macron, will face the French public once again, seeking re-election in 2022. Will he be able to storm back to the Elysee Palace? Seems unlikely.

The incumbent president had very low approval ratings in 2020, a little over 40 per cent.[79] Macron was destined to preside over France when they were going through one of the toughest phases in recent times. The discontentment against Macron's presidency has arisen due to many factors. He is seen as pro-rich and lacking in empathy;[80] and he struggled to bring the country together during the coronavirus pandemic. He has also grappled with recurring terror attacks. And most importantly, France has been through its worst economic crisis since World War II during his tenure.

Macron's planets are not looking favourable, either. A debilitated Neptune will transit his third house during election time in 2022, denoting disappointments and leadership failure.

[79] Paul Taylor, 'Macron Needs an Economic Miracle to Save His Presidency', *POLITICO*, 14 July 2020, https://www.politico.eu/article/french-president-emmanuel-macron-needs-an-economic-miracle-to-save-his-presidency/.

[80] Rym Momtaz, 'What Macron Can Learn from Biden', *POLITICO*, 15 November 2020, https://www.politico.eu/article/what-macron-could-learn-from-biden/.

Even the transiting Uranus will be debilitated in his fourth house, implying that he will see failure in his own country. This indicates that there are minimal chances for Macron to be re-elected.

His most likely competitor, Marine Le Pen, president of the National Rally Political Party, a far-right populist candidate has a better planetary transits during 2022. Her Pluto will be exalted in the fifth house of the government, showing that she will have a say in the formation of the government or, perhaps, she will become the president herself.

Moreover, Planet-X will also be transiting into her tenth house of career, indicating an apparent elevation in her status. Add to that, Marine also has an exalted Uranus. She is a serious threat for Emmanuel Macron. Thus the signs indicate that we will see a new president of France in 2022. Surprisingly, France has never had a woman president so far. Probably Pluto's exaltation after seventy years will bring that change.

Prediction #34

Can Kamal Haasan Become the Chief Minister of Tamil Nadu?

I have always been a Kamal Haasan fan. Besides his exceptional acting skills, I have always felt there is a sweet naivety about him. His personality is a combination of Libra and Pisces, and his horoscope confirms this fact. While he is amazingly artistic and creative, he genuinely wants to do something for the society and the people too.

Meanwhile, Rajinikanth is smart and astute, a quintessential Scorpio–Sagittarius–Capricorn. He clearly assessed that he didn't have any chance to become the chief minister, and used Covid-19 as an opportunity to come out of the situation he had created for himself.[81]

---

[81] 'Rajinikanth Announces He's Quitting Politics with a Letter to Fans', *MW*, https://www.mansworldindia.com/more/news/politics/Rajinikanthh-announces-hes-quitting-politics-with-a-letter-to-fans/, accessed 12 March 2021.

Both Kamal Haasan and Rajinikanth have exceptional horoscopes, which made them great superstars. I always wondered if either of the two had it in them to become the next M.G. Ramachandran, Ronald Reagan or Jayalalithaa. When I examined their horoscopes, I felt neither could do that. While a nascent exalted Neptune in the first house has made Kamal Haasan the legend he is, a nascent Pluto exalted in the first house has made Rajinikanth this remarkable phenomenon.

A person needs to have a powerful seventh house, besides all the other planets, to make them the head of government. Ronald Reagan, M.G. Ramachandran, and Jayalalithaa had that. Kamal Haasan doesn't have any strong planet in the seventh house and hence won't catapult to the topmost position in the state. Rajinikanth had better planets in the seventh house. He had Uranus, the seventh lord in exaltation, transiting his eleventh house, which indicates that he could become more powerful as he grows older. Despite that, Rajinikanth has gone out of the race If he, with his strong planets connected to seventh house, couldn't do it, Kamal Haasan certainly can't.

This undeniably shows that Dravidian politics is not that easy. This means Kamal Haasan will never become the chief minister. But he will be a significant influencer and his party will have an important voice. He may even forced to form alliances with others if he needs to stay relevant. Even if he doesn't have it in him to be the king, he can certainly become a kingmaker. Meanwhile here, too, Rajini may beat him. His Uranus shows that he will be better at that job. And so it goes. And I'm still a Kamal fan!

Prediction #35

Vijay or Ajith? Who Has Better Chances in Politics?

An actor working in the Tamil film industry can always prepare for a career in politics as a retirement plan. If the people of Tamil Nadu like you and make you their hero, then they may put you on such a high pedestal that you can take a shot at ruling them in real life besides the silver screen. Connections to the film world as an author or a writer could help too. C.N. Annadurai, M. Karunanidhi, M.G. Ramachandran, V.N. Janaki and Jayalalitha, all these past chief ministers had filmi connections. It goes without saying that these leaders had brilliant horoscopes which reflect their strong careers.

With Rajinikanth out of the fray and Kamal Haasan being the lone ranger, all eyes are now on the younger superstars—Vijay and Ajith. Does either of the two have it in him to be a the chief minister?

Vijay has a fantastic horoscope as far as his acting career goes. All the four planets—Chiron, Planet-X, Planet-Y and Planet-Z are in strong postions, making him a top-notch actor and a superstar, the 'ilayathalapathy' or a young lieutenant for the Tamils. He has all the attributes of a good politician. The Gemini–Cancerian has remarkable communication skills; he is a smooth talker, with great relationship skills. He ensures he is everyone's favourite. But will that be enough to make him successful in politics?

Besides other factors that ensure success in show biz, success in the political arena depends upon the seventh house. All successful actors-turned-politicians have a powerful seventh house. Unfortunately, Vijay has a weak seventh house. His seventh lord, Neptune, is in debilitation, which suggests failure in politics. He could get embroiled in unwanted controversies and power struggles.

Ajith Kumar, the other young superstar, has a strong seventh house with his seventh lord, Uranus, exalted in the eleventh house. This is the exact position of the planet in the birth chart of Justin Trudeau, the Canadian prime minister, who was born in the same year as Ajith. Ajith also has Pluto, the fourth lord, forming a power centre with Uranus in conjunction in the second house. The fourth house indicates homeland and local governance, and Ajith Kumar stands a better chance of governing a state or performing better in the political arena than Vijay.

Prediction #36

Will Baba Ramdev Continue to Make News?

Baba Ramdev was born two days before Salman Khan and, like him, is probably one of the most famous bachelors in India.

Baba has Neptune, the ninth lord, in exaltation, giving him a spiritual connection. He also has Chiron, his ascendant lord, exalted in the eighth house, making him the yoga master. The strongest planet of his chart, Pluto, is nestled in the second house, making him a business tycoon.

Ramdev's planets look very powerful in the future too. The deeply exalted fifth lord, Pluto, will transit into his seventh house of politics and public life. The spiritual guru formed a political party a decade ago and his political interests will grow stronger in the coming years. The fifth house indicates the media, and his relationship with the media will continue to be strong, as Pluto, his fifth lord, is getting exalted. Neptune also transits into his ninth house, indicating that Baba's spiritual relevance will also grow.

Baba has a weak Uranus in the second house. This has resulted in the several controversies his company, Patanjali, has been through. The run-ins he and the organisation has had with the law are very similar to Salman Khan's, due to the presence of Venus and Mars in conjunction in the seventh house. The company, Patanjali Ayurved Limited, was established in 2006, when Planet-X was in deep exaltation, but at the same time, Pluto had just gone into nascent debilitation. Hence the dichotomy. Its growth has been massive—its revenue was ₹25,000 crore in 2020,[82] in just

---

[82]   PTI, 'Patanjali Group Eyes Rs 25k Crore Turnover in FY20', *The Economic Times*, 24 January 2020, https://economictimes.indiatimes.com/industry/cons-products/fmcg/patanjali-group-eyes-rs-25k-crore-turnover-in-fy20/articleshow/73581643.cms?from=mdr.

its fifteenth year of existence. But it has been courting numerous legal cases too.[83]

Baba Ramdev claims his company will replace Hindustan Unilever (HUL) as the number one FMCG company in the country. Is that possible? It's unlikely. Hindustan Unilever has a better date of establishment compared to Patanjali. HUL has also transformed itself continuously, during its strategic years in more than eighty years of existence in India. Patanjali Ayurved will grow huge in its own way, but becoming the number one FMCG company will remain a distant dream.

Meanwhile, Baba's weak Uranus denotes that the company's controversies will continue. Uranus is associated with business in Ramdev's horoscope. Patanjali will see large fluctuations in its fortunes due to this. At different points of time, it has been at the centre of allegations regarding wrongdoings, false claims and labour law violations. But, irrespective of Ramdev's business dealings, his legacy, influence and impact will remain strong.

Prediction #37

The Next Era of the Ambanis

While there are Godrejs, Hindujas, Adanis, Tatas and Birlas, the Ambanis are the most prominent newsmakers. Their new residences and marriages have made news as much as their family feuds.

Though Mukesh Ambani, the head of India's largest conglomerate, shies away from the limelight, he continues to make waves without saying anything himself—he became the

---

[83] Jagpreet Singh Sandhu, 'Criminal Complaint Filed against Baba Ramdev, Patanjali Ayurved in Chandigarh Court for Attempt to Murder, Sale of Adulterated Drugs', *The Indian Express*, 27 June 2020, https://indianexpress.com/article/cities/chandigarh/criminal-complaint-filed-against-baba-ramdev-patanjali-ayurved-in-chandigarh-court-for-attempt-to-murder-sale-of-adulterated-drugs-6478247/.

richest Asian,[84] and has wealth that is twice that of the second-richest Asians, the Kwoks of Hong Kong. The question is, how long can he personally, and the group as a whole, keep going on?

Reliance Industries went through a huge crisis when the founder Dhirubhai Ambani's sons fought over the control of the group companies after the death of their father. It was a significant moment in the history of the company when the brothers separated, after a very public feud.

If an organisation is founded on an astrologically sound date, and is then reorganised on a bad date, it can be a disastrous change. But conversely, a company can grow from strength to strength if it is reorganised during good times. Fortunately for Reliance Industries, October 2005, when the company came into its current form and realigned its businesses, was perhaps the best time in about fifty years. There was an extraordinary alignment of planets, with eight planets in strong positions. The Ambanis were fortunate that their company was reborn at a time when the planets were in such a rare, fortuitous combination that may occur again only after a century. Knowingly or unknowingly, Reliance was restructured at the most opportune time possible.

Then, why did Anil Ambani go through such harrowing times? Why did his group of companies sink to such depths? Anil Ambani is a Grey Lizard. Pluto was in a very strong position during the time of restructuring, and it couldn't have favoured him. Simple.

Mukesh Ambani's group got a shot in the arm because it was reborn in 2005. While Dhirubhai was the hero of the story of Reliance from 1966 until he passed away in 2002, Mukesh's story truly starts from 2005 onwards. And looking at the planetary positions in 2005, it is no surprise that Reliance has grown multiple times since then.

---

[84] 'Asia's 20 Richest Families Control $463 Billion', *Bloomberg Wealth*, 29 November 2020, https://www.bloomberg.com/features/2020-asia-richest-families/.

If we want to look at the future, we need to look at the horoscopes of Mukesh and Nita Ambani's children. At age 23, Nita Ambani was told by doctors that she could not conceive naturally[85]. After seven years of marriage, in 1991, twins Akash and Isha were born via in-vitro fertilisation. This is interesting because if Akash and Isha were born before 1990, Pluto wouldn't have been in its own house and they would have lost on the power of the most powerful planet in the universe. Probably it was destined to be that way so that Pluto will power Reliance to grow more prominent through the next generation of the Ambanis.

Prediction #38
Will Gautam Adani Be Able to Keep Flying High?

Gautam Adani's resume looks impressive. He started as a humble commodity trader in 1988 and went on to build a huge conglomerate. While the entire world was reeling under the impact of Covid-19, in 2020, he added a jaw-dropping $ 35 billion[86] to his riches. He is now the second richest Indian and closing in on Mukesh Ambani. Would his growth story continue? Yes, but with huge roadblocks.

The company was incorporated in the year 1993 and came with a public issue in 1994. Pluto and Neptune were in the strongest positions in these two years and the company's tremendous growth and status can be attributed to that.

Looking further, some milestones aren't encouraging astrologically. In August 2006, the company was renamed Adani Enterprises Limited from Adani Exports. Pluto just got into nascent debilitation and Neptune was deeply debilitated during this time. While the massive placement of Planet-X and Uranus can push the company into good positions, the biggest planets

---

85   https://www.dnaindia.com/entertainment/report-at-23-nita-ambani-was-told-she-could-never-conceive-akash-and-isha-ambani-were-born-via-ivf-2739697

86   https://economictimes.indiatimes.com/news/company/corporate-trends/from-a-commodities-trader-to-indias-second-wealthiest-person-the-incredible-story-of-gautam-adani/articleshow/81680774.cms?from=mdr

Pluto and Neptune in weak positions probably indicate a weak foundation.

Adani Power was started in 1996, a good year according to astrology. Other projects, like IT and data centre, which started post 2019 will not have much trouble as they were started when Pluto was in strong positions. The troubles will originate from businesses started during 2010-2017.

When you dig deep and go into the dates when the various subsidiary companies of the group were established, there seems to be a long, challenging road ahead. The biggest money spinners for the group—Adani Ports & SEZ, Adani Green Energy, Adani Transmission, Adani Infrastructure— were established during 2010-2017 when Pluto got deeper and deeper into debilitation.

So, can Gautam Adani go on to be the richest man in India? Yes, it is possible. He has almost nine planets in dignity in his horoscope, and he can do that. Albeit that could just be temporary. Despite the presence of strong planets in his horoscope, there are two important yet weak planets in his chart—Uranus in fall and Pluto is almost in the Grey Lizard avatar. His growth story can be pretty impressive till 2025, when Pluto would push him further. But during 2025-29 when Pluto will get into the Grey Lizard zone and Uranus would get debilitated, Adani will get into some serious troubles with his businesses.

It is difficult to predict the kind of challenges Adani group would face at this point of time but just like the huge roadblock for their coal project in Australia since 2010[87] they will get into more and more troubles. Gautam's businesses will face various obstacles and his financial empire would just get saddled with many troubles, legal wrangles and financial muddles.

Interestingly, Gautam's son Karan Adani who manages the Adani Ports too is a Grey Lizard with Pluto in deep debilitation.

---

[87] https://www.boomlive.in/fact-file/why-are-australians-protesting-against-adani-group-10872

This just confirms the fact that the huge conglomerate of Adani has huge challenges ahead which is contradictory to the promises the group shows in 2021.

Prediction #39

Will Elon Musk Deliver on His Promises?

Business magnate Elon Musk loves to put up a show. With his Moon in Leo, he loves to do things in style. Morever, his out-of-the-box ideas can be attributed to his Sun and Mercury being in Gemini. The question is, will he be able to deliver on his promises?

Musk has a fantastic horoscope, with a strong Pluto and an exalted Uranus in conjunction in the third house of the mind. He is a brilliant engineer and designer as he has Planet-Y in exaltation in the tenth house. Planet-Z in its own second house makes him one of the richest men in the world. He became the richest for a week in 2021 before giving back the crown to Jeff Bezos.[88] The second question is, how wealthy will he become and how long will he be able to sustain it?

Elon Musk has a strong third house that indicates movement, vehicles and transportation. His Tesla products and businesses of all the modes of vehicular transport, will do really well. His ideas on the alternative sources of energy, and renewable energy, will be ground-breaking and help a lot in the transportation of the future. And his radical ideas on liquid-energy fuel that even power spaceships, are extraordinary and commendable.

Musk, however, has a weak ninth house. His ninth lord, Neptune, is in debilitation in his fifth house and will remain debilitated for the entire 2020s in his ninth house of luck and 'long' travels. Interestingly, though his third house of short

---

[88] Lisette Voytko, 'Jeff Bezos Once Again the World's Richest Person after Rollercoaster Week', *Forbes*, 16 January 2021, https://www.forbes.com/sites/lisettevoytko/2021/01/16/jeff-bezos-once-again-the-worlds-richest-person-after-rollercoaster-week/?sh=2c19ffa3175d.

travels is positive, his ninth house is negative. His biggest failures will come in the area of space exploration. His idea of colonisation of Mars is unlikely to take off as the 'long' travel planet is weak during this time.

The 'long' travel-based businesses owned by Elon Musk's other company, Space-X, will fall short of expectations. Uranus will also remain in debilitation during 2026–2030, indicating that the timelines he has promised for the missions to Mars will largely remain unsuccessful.

Space-X will do astonishingly well in many areas, but will also backtrack on its ideas and proposals multiple times. Expect the plan for Mars to be revised time and again. The ideas may finally be implemented, but not in Musk's lifetime.

That brings us to the third question—will Elon Musk be able to hold on to his position as the richest or second richest person in the world?

That will be very difficult. Though he has a very strong Planet-Z and his Saturn is in the second and eleventh houses, they aren't strong enough. Planets higher in the hierarchy, such as Uranus, Neptune or Pluto, in these houses would have ensured that he continued accumulating riches. People like Bill Gates or Warren Buffett stayed on the list of the richest persons for long, as they had Pluto or other stronger planets in the 2–11 quadrants. Billionaires born during 1964–1967 have stronger chances to stay on top, ahead of the Elon Musk's slightly volatile planets.

Meanwhile, expect Musk to continue to court controversies with his sweeping and exaggerated statements.[89] Geminians can be brilliant communicators, but some of them are known for their big gaffes. Add the Leo portion to that, and it can be an interesting mix. A Gemini–Leo can sometimes go too far from reality, and when it doesn't work out, can come up

[89] Peter Cohan, 'Musk's Exaggerations Endanger Tesla Stockholders', *Forbes*, 3 August 2017, https://www.forbes.com/sites/petercohan/2017/08/03/musks-exaggerations-endanger-tesla-stockholders/?sh=7125ad6b5db6.

with some interesting digression from the original idea. Donald Trump was another Geminian who used to go back and forth on his own statements. If Musk doesn't control his urge to go overboard, then the danger of him being seen as a person like Trump, albeit a more intelligent one, still lurks. We need to learn to take Mr Musk's projections and promises with more than a pinch of salt—probably discount 40 per cent of what he says, and then we should have the right estimates.

Prediction #40
What Will Happen to Facebook and Mark Zuckerberg?

Something is going to happen to Facebook. Something drastic, something unbelievable, something radical. Mark Zuckerberg has complete control over it, with over 60 per cent of the shares still with him.[90] It may not be so much longer.

Zuckerberg was born on an auspicious full-moon day, with Uranus and Neptune in exaltation. Planet-Z was also in nascent exaltation making it powerful horoscope indeed.

Interestingly, on 4 February 2004, when Mark Zuckerberg set up Facebook, five planets were exactly in opposite positions to what he has in his birth chart. Neptune is in exaltation in his birth chart, but it was in debilitation when Facebook was founded. Planet-X was in deep exaltation, while the same planet is in debilitation in his horoscope. The same was applicable for Mars, Venus, Jupiter and Chiron. The only two planets which were powerfully placed, and in sync with the horoscope, were Uranus and Planet-Z.

Now, this is intriguing, because most of the forces, during the time when Zuckerberg established the company, were against him. This means Facebook has grown beyond Mark Zuckerberg's control. It could either fell him or fall into the

---

90   Jason Aten, 'Why Facebook's Biggest Problem Isn't Fake News or Privacy. It's Mark Zuckerberg', *Inc.*, https://www.inc.com/jason-aten/why-facebooks-biggest-problem-isnt-fake-news-or-privacy-its-mark-zuckerberg.html, accessed 12 March 2021.

hands of someone else. Uranus and Planet-Z have given him all the benefits and riches, and have made him one of the top five billionaires in the world. But the rest of the planets will revolt against him, and there could be a different kind of an end to the Facebook story.

His weakly-placed Planet-Y has already affronted him with several legal and congressional issues. Privacy concerns, while using Facebook, have become a huge issue, but they are just one part of the problem. It is only a matter of time before the rest of the planets create additional trouble. Mark Zuckerberg has invited some twenty experts to look into the issues at Facebook to set things straight.[91] But this may not be enough to save him from other serious crises that may arise at Facebook in the 2020s.

The most significant planet, placed exactly opposite, is the most powerful planet in the universe— the boss, Pluto. Pluto will enter Zuckerberg's third house of the mind, indicating that Zuckerberg will go through a lot of headaches, worries and frustration. The third house also indicates leadership, and the most significant change that can happen is a change in leadership at Facebook.

Zuckerberg has decided to give 99 per cent of his wealth to charity, which is one big factor that will save him. If he hadn't pledged the money to charity, then a lot of it might have been snatched away from him. By pledging to charity he has brought a positive manifestation upon himself, knowingly or unknowingly.

Prediction #41

The 'Non' Ambani

Don't let the fiery speech of Anant Ambani, the youngest child of Mukesh Ambani, at the fortieth annual general meeting

---

[91] Steven Levy, 'Facebook Names the 20 People Who Can Overrule Mark Zuckerberg', *Wired*, 5 June 2020, https://www.wired.com/story/facebook-names-20-people-overrule-mark-zuckerberg/.

(AGM) of Reliance fool you.[92] He isn't as aggressive as he happears to be.

The Ambanis have always been very powerful, not just financially but also from an emotional perspective. Dhirubhai Ambani, the patriarch from whom the family derives inspiration and values, was a combination of the ambitious Sagittarius and the strong-willed Scorpio. Mukesh and Anil have planets in the controlling and dominating Aries. Neither could have been subservient to the other, which eventually led to their separation.

Even the matriarch of the Mukesh Ambani family, Nita Ambani, is a combination of the suave Libra and strong Aries. Anant's elder siblings, Isha and Akash, the twins, have the same combination of signs as their mother—Libra-Aries. The entire family consists of strong, powerful personalities. For Anant, Mukesh and Nita Ambani's youngest child, being born with a sweet combination of a Cancer–Pisces is a deviation from the 'strong' Ambani family. Cancerians make good business people, no question about that, but the drive to make billions comes to a Cancerian mostly when they don't have the billions. Pisceans hate to go out in the corporate jungle, hunting for money. Anant would hate hunting of any sort. He is an animal lover and runs a shelter for injured animals and animals in distress.[93] He is naturally soft-spoken and kind-hearted—as his mother says. And from an astrological perspective too, Anant Ambani he is a 'non' Ambani.

Thankfully for Anant, he is the youngest in the family. Akash and Isha will lead from the front, and he will secretly be glad that he isn't the eldest. While Akash and Isha proudly carry the mantle of being the Ambanis, he doesn't need to be the face of the company which would otherwise have put a huge pressure on him.

[92] 'Anant Ambani Speech at Reliance 40 years', *YouTube*, 25 December 2017, https://www.youtube.com/watch?v=ymHSVlySxC8.

[93] 'Exotic Pets of the Rich and Famous', *The Economic Times*, 4 March 2015, https://economictimes.indiatimes.com/magazines/panache/exotic-pets-of-the-rich-and-famous/articleshow/46452286.cms?from=mdr.

But does that mean Anant's life is going to be uninteresting? Far from it. Anant's interestingly placed planets in the eleventh house show that he will be a philanthropist. In that case, Mukesh Ambani might decide to do something similar to the Bill and Melinda Gates Foundation, and there may be no better person to lead that initiative than Anant. Anant will show the world that the Ambanis have a heart too, and that even philanthropy can be done systematically, helping millions change their lives.

Expect Anant to broker peace between the warring factions of his family. The Cancer–Pisces will play a significant role in bringing the family closer. Expect more camaraderie between the older brothers and their family in the coming years. Meanwhile, Anant will learn to relax and ease the pressure of being an Ambani on himself.

Prediction #42
Will Rahul Dravid Coach the Senior Team Too?

The news that Rahul Dravid will take over as the interim head coach of the Indian team visiting Sri Lanka in July 2021, in the absence of Ravi Shastri, has gladdened many Indian hearts. Just the possibility of a glimpse of the legend once again around the cricket pitch is a thrilling idea to Indian cricket-fans. So how good will Rahul Dravid be as the coach of the senior Indian cricket team?

Dravid could have taken an easy and more financially rewarding route coaching a cash-rich IPL or an international team. But Dravid's priorities have always been clear—country first. Even after quitting the game, he took a tougher route coaching the Indian Under-19 cricket team.

Rahul is a combination of the intelligent Sagittarius and the wise Pisces. With Dravid as its coach and mentor, the Under-19 Indian team has won a World Cup and reached the finals of another.

He is akin to a factory churning good player – Prithvi Shaw, Shubman Gill, Mayank Agarwal, the list goes on.

Dravid is the director at the National Cricket Academy (NCA) in Bangalore, since 2019. Will he become the head coach of the Indian team anytime? Yes, it seem likely to happen soon. Rahul Dravid has a brilliant horoscope with Pluto, his third lord, in conjunction with the deeply exalted Uranus in his ascendant. Uranus is his sixth lord and he has been doing all the dirty jobs always. He stood as 'the wall,' taking all the blows on his body as an opener or coming one-down besides keeping wickets, if required. Now all of this happened during his playing days. Interestingly, he also has a very strong ninth lord Planet-X in exaltation in his eleventh house. The ninth house represents a coach or a guru, and the eleventh house stands for the second half of life.

This kind of an arrangement is very similar to football legend Zinedine Zidane's horoscope. Zidane was exceptional for his country, during his playing days and has been a successful coach. This simply indicates that Rahul Dravid will go on to be one of the best coaches to come from India ever. Hopefully, Rahul Dravid will keep his coaching successes reserved for the Indian team. It seems Indian cricket can look forward to some glorious days ahead. A World Cup win with the senior team? Possible, very possible.

Prediction #43
Can Virat Kohli Win a Cricket World Cup as a Captain?

Fans in India and Argentina have one frustration in common. Their country's captain hasn't won them the cup that matters. Interestingly, both Messi and Virat Kohli have two great chances to have a shot at redeeming glory for their country. And it seems Kohli has as good a chance as Messi, if not better.

It is almost as if Virat Kohli's legacy is at stake. He has already won two World Cups—one as the Under-19 World Cup captain in 2008, and the other in 2011 when Dhoni won the One Day International (ODI) World Cup for India. But Kohli hasn't won a World Cup as the captain of the senior men's team, and that's the cup that matters. In fact Virat Kohli hasn't won any ICC tournament as a captain , at the time of this book going to press, in early June. Yet while this article is being written in May 2021. He has a realistic chance to win the ICC Test Championship in July 2021. Even if he wins that fans would still compare him to Dhoni. Somehow it is essential to win a World Cup in either the T20 or ODI formats.

Realistically, Virat Kohli has got three chances for doing that. We will see all of them one by one.

50 over World Cup in 2023 in India

This quadrennial event is the most prestigious tournament in the world of cricket. There is a logical sequence to the the winning team captain's year of birth. The last six events were won by the captains born 1965, 1974, 1974, 1981, 1981 & 1986. Only the greatest captains with the best horoscopes, born during exceptional years when the planets were in the strongest position, can win a 50-over World Cup. Astrologically, the next year in this sequence would be 1990. Virat Kohli was not born in 1990 and hence his chances to win the 2023 50-over World Cup are zilch.

T20 World Cup in 2022 in Australia

The years 2021-2022 belongs to captains born during 1986-87. Uranus would be transiting Aries during this time and is exalted there. Captains born during 1986-87 have Uranus in deepest exaltation. Besides, they also have Neptune in deep exaltation. Additionally, Neptune too would be in its own house during 2021-22 having just entered into its nascent state. This would add to the strengths of the captain's born during 1986-87. So, there is an excellent chance that a 1986-

87-born captain would win the 2022 T20 World Cup to be played in Australia.

I have written an entire book to show that Virat Kohli was indeed born during 1986-87 and not in 1988. He is one of the captains with a great chance to win the tournament. So, while Virat Kohli + has a chance to win, so can any other 1986-87 born captain. That could even be Australian captain Aaron Finch. Full Moon-Finch hasn't won a huge tournament yet and he has been through major challenges during 2019-20 with his own batting performances. This could be a good chance for him to win the cup and redeem himself. But there is another man looming large on the horizon, literally. Kieron Pollard! The 1987-born Kieron Pollard, the captain of West Indies, can just sneak under the nose of all and win the tournament.

T20 World Cup in 2021, in India or UAE

Virat Kohli has the best chance to win this tournament as captain. He would have the home advantage, unless the tournament is shifted to UAE due to Covid. The current T20 team looks extraordinary, with at least two players good enough to play at one spot. Astrologically, all the players, starting from KL Rahul at the top to Jasprit Bumrah at number 11, could create the best astrologically balanced team to come from India in a long time. Virat Kohli will never get a better chance to win the tournament than this.

The reverse of the above two events can happen. Aaron Finch can win the 2021 World Cup in India, and Virat Kohli can make it poetically even by going and winning in Australia in 2022. Finally, both these captains have the best chance to win the 2021 and 2022 T20 World Cups. That simply means that Virat Kohli will definitely not retire before he becomes a legend.

Prediction #44

Will Messi Ever Win a Major Tournament for Argentina?

If we have spoken about Virat Kohli, can Lionel Messi be far behind? There is an extraordinary parallel between these two, who are the greatest players of their respective sports. Both were born a year apart; both are exceptional players—the best in the world; and both have not won any prominent tournament for their countries till early June 2021.

I need to answer one question that football fans keep asking me—will Messi ever win a big tournament for Argentina? The answer is yes. He will.

Messi has been a true legend in club football. He has spent his entire professional career with Barcelona, and has won a record twenty-three trophies for them. These include—ten La Liga titles, four UEFA Champions Leagues, and six Copas Del Reys. He has already won the Ballon d'Or, the greatest recognition in football, a record six times. But one thing that really haunts Messi and all his fans is that he hasn't won a major title for his country, Argentina.

There are some patches of years when some of the greatest players are born, and they go on to achieve the greatest accolades in their sports. In recent times, those years were 1981 legend and then 1986–1987. The 1981-born Iker Casillas won the 2010 World Cup and two European Championship titles for Spain. The 1986-born Hugo Lloris, the France captain, won the 2018 World Cup. Incidentally, I predicted these triumphs. Messi was born in 1987, with Uranus in the deepest exaltation in his horoscope. Uranus will remain exalted till 2024. He has not won the World Cup as a captain is perhaps because the football gods wanted to be fair. They made Lionel Messi the best player on earth, and gave the World Cups to Iker Casillas and Hugo Lloris. The same set of planets can't win you everything, you see.

But then there is the world's 'other' best player, who has also won a major title for his country—Cristiano Ronaldo. And there lies the hope for Lionel Messi to win at least one major title for his country. Let's face it. Lionel Messi was not born to win a World Cup as a captain. A younger player born in the 1990's will win the tournament. Period. There is a karmic quota for players born in any year, and the patch of 1986–1987 has already won theirs and there cannot be one more from amongst them. But then, he could win a Copa America.

Between 1981 and 1986, the patch 1983–1985 has some strong planetary positions which can make a player win the second- or third-most important tournaments, such as the Euro Cup or the Copa America. Cristiano Ronaldo, a 1985-born, won the Euro Cup. Winning the Euro Cup is not a small deal; it is the second biggest tournament in the world. But actually, the captain who won the Euro Cup that day was Nani, a 1986-born, who captained the Portugal team when Ronaldo was injured.

Another good year was 1983. The Brazil captain, Dani Alves, and the Chile captain, Claudio Bravio, both were born in 1983 and won the last three Copa America titles between them. Well, here is the opportunity, a huge opportunity. If the last Copa America was won by a 1983-born captain, the next one should be won by a 1986–1987-born captain as that is the logical progression of the planetary influence. That's where Lionel Messi comes in. There will be two Copa Americas held during this period and, mark my words, Lionel Messi will positively win one of them.

Does Messi have any competition? Yes, he does. There are two captains—born in this patch of 1986–1987, who also have a chance to win the coveted tournament. Captains Radamel Falcao of Columbia and Diego Godin of Uruguay, both born in 1986 also have a chance to win the coveted tournament. So, it is actually between Columbia and Argentina now. There are two shots at glory and Messi should be able to clinch atleast one of the two Copa America tournaments to be held in 2021 or 2024. Finally, the long painful wait for Messi fans should be over.

Prediction #45
Can Neymar Win the Football World Cup for Brazil?

In 2018, Kaushik Bagchi, a very senior banker I worked with during my days in the insurance industry, was extremely upset when I predicted that Brazil would not win the World Cup. I reasoned that according to astrology, the World Cup victory is dependent on the team captain's horoscope. He said, 'Football means Brazil and Brazil means football vice versa. No other country can win the World Cup. How does it matter who the captain is?'

Well, it does matter. The captain is the most important person in a football match, besides the coach. And, the captain's horoscope will decide if your country will win the highest glory in a sport or not.

The achievements in sports and politics are manifested by the seventh house, which also indicates the public enemy. The public enemies of politicians and sports stars are known to everyone. Narendra Modi has Planet-X in deep exaltation in his seventh house. M.S. Dhoni has Neptune in nascent exaltation in the same house. Rohit Sharma has Uranus in exaltation in his seventh house. This is the reason they are the champions in their respective fields.

A player can have a higher hierarchy planet such as Planet-X, Uranus, Neptune or Pluto in exaltation or in its own house in the seventh house, or as the seventh lord. We can then assume that there is a higher chance for the player to be a champion. At the same time, if a strong planet is debilitated, or in fall in the seventh house, or if the seventh lord is debilitated, then the opposite would be true.

Unfortunately, I don't have good news for Neymar and Brazil fans. Neymar has Pluto in the first house, which makes him a great football player. He doesn't have the astrological star power to captain a team to glory. His fifth lord, Neptune, is exalted, making him one of the most famous footballers in the world. Moreover, the Brazilian footballer has no planet in the seventh house, and the seventh lord, Planet-X, is in fall in the first house. This is a very shocking placement that indicates situations where Neymar would almost single-handedly win a tournament for his country since all the other planets are strong. But he can't cross the last hurdle because of the placement of his Planet-X.

Then, could he play under a captain who could win the World Cup? Yes, that's possible. A weak seventh house indicates that Neymar would fail as a captain, but his other planets are so powerfully placed that he can be a part of a World Cup-winning team. That means Brazil has a chance to win the World Cup only if some other player captains them.

True Brazil is football. But even football needs a captain with a solid seventh house to win the World Cup.

Prediction #46
After Dhoni, Who?

Dhoni is one of the most celebrated cricketers in India. He has carved out a legacy that very few would be able to match. A World Cup triumph; T20 World Cup win; an ICC Champions Trophy win; taking India to the top of the charts in Tests and ODIs; several Indian Premier League (IPL) wins; and even a few Champions League laurels—the victories he has brought to India is phenomenal. It will take a great player to beat his record.

So far, Virat Kohli, Dhoni's successor, doesn't seem likely to do that. The closest he came to Dhoni was reaching the finals of the Champions Trophy in 2017, only to lose ignominiously to Pakistan in the final. He led India to the semi-finals of the ICC World Cup in 2019. Perhaps Virat has another three or four years to accomplish what Dhoni did. But it doesn't seem he can emulate Dhoni, as he has fewer shots at the tournaments now. He would have two attempts at T20 World Cups in 2021 and 2022, a Test Championship in 2021, a fifty-over World Cup in 2023. He needs to win one of each of the formats to be called a true successor to Dhoni. As we have discussed in the earlier chapter, prima facie, it doesn't appear he would be able to do that.

Is there someone else who could have done it for India? Rohit Sharma was probably the best Indian captain we never had. He has a better horoscope than Virat Kohli. But, unfortunately, he has never led India in any key tournament. India has lost at least two ICC tournaments, because Rohit Sharma wasn't at the helm of affairs. India's loss has been Mumbai Indians' gain, and Rohit has already won numerous titles for them.

There is another superbly talented cricketer, an opener, a sweet timer of the ball, sensible, calm and mature, a team man who can bat according to the circumstances—similar to Rohit Sharma. His horoscope is also as powerful as Rohit Sharma's, or maybe even a shade better. And this player also can bring home a World Cup or two and a couple of ICC tournament titles as a captain. And that one cricketer who can do a Dhoni, has to be K.L. Rahul.

K.L. Rahul has an extraordinary horoscope, with Pluto and Neptune in the strongest positions. While Pluto makes him a great batsman, Neptune can make him a successful leader with a Midas touch, similar to Dhoni. Dhoni has Neptune in nascent exaltation in the seventh house, while Rahul has his seventh lord Neptune in deepest exaltation. These are comparable placements. The sooner K.L. Rahul is groomed to take over the captaincy from Virat Kohli, the better it will be for India. Rahul will win major tournaments starting 2021 and can even go on to win World Cups till the early 2030s.

There is something curious about Rahul's career. He was considered an excellent prospect for Test cricket in his initial days, but there were doubts regarding his potential in the shorter formats. In the first prediction I wrote about him in 2015, I predicted he would play exceedingly well in the shorter formats[94]. I said he would play for India and be successful in the IPL. With his planets in place, K.L. Rahul will do well even in Test cricket.

But his biggest achievement will come as a captain. He has already received the vice-captaincy band a couple of times. It is just a matter of time before he assumes leadership. As captain, Rahul's planets, Pluto and Neptune, will exercise their full powers, and he will bring many trophies for India.

There are not many cricketers of Rahul's age who have such a good set of planets. Virat has enough competition. That's all the more reason why Rahul will be a successful captain.

So, now you know who should be leading India in the 2023 World Cup, right?

Predictions #47

A Cricket Superstar in the Making

As an Indian cricket fan and an astrologer, one of the biggest regrets I have for Indian cricket is regarding Rohit Sharma. If I could change one thing about Indian cricket in the last decade, it would be to make Rohit Sharma the Indian ODI or T20 teams captain. Rohit Sharma has the best horoscope amongst all captains globally. Coupled with luck, he could have easily led India to at least one World Cup victory, if not two.

Another Indian cricketer player with a similar story is Shreyas Iyer. I hope that history doesn't repeat itself, and he can rise to captaincy whenever the time is right. Shreyas has Planet-X, the seventh lord in exaltation, besides Pluto in its own house and Neptune in exaltation. Now that is a powerhouse of

---

94 Greenstone Lobo, 'KL Rahul Will Serve Indian Cricket for Many Years', *DNA*, 10 January 2015, https://www.dnaindia.com/sports/column-kl-rahul-will-serve-indian-cricket-for-many-years-2051296.

a chart. He will be a great player, playing some extraordinary innings for India because Pluto would be traversing his third house of the hands during the 2020s. He will have Neptune in the fifth house of fame, popularity and extraordinary successes, signifying many success stories to unfold. He will be a part of some impressive wins.

Planet-X is the key here. The seventh house is all about leadership and victory over your enemies. For Shreyas Iyer, the seventh lord, Planet-X, will be exalted for a very long time. If India doesn't use that benefit, then Delhi Capitals will use it in IPL, which would be ironic for Indian cricket. Winning the IPL as a captain is a significant achievement. If you win a title, you dilute your karmic quota for any important future tournament like a World Cup.

In the mid-2020s, after Virat Kohli retires and Rohit Sharma moves on, K.L. Rahul will take centre stage and probably become the captain of the Indian cricket team. In that case, K.L. Rahul could lead India in one or two formats and Shreyas Iyer in at least another. Doing so will enhance the chances of India winning more tournaments.

India is fortunate that K.L. Rahul has a powerful seventh house with exalted Neptune in transit, resulting in many wins. But even the legendary M.S. Dhoni couldn't win all the World Cups because he was the only captain for India during his time. Besides, he also diluted his karmic quota by winning for Chennai Super Kings. Hopefully, the powers at BCCI will not allow it in future and give India the maximum opportunities to win tournaments by making Shreyas a captain.

Predictions #48
How Good Will These GenNext Cricketers Be ?

The web magazine the *Cricket Monthly* by ESPNcricinfo conferred with fifteen experts—international coaches, players, scouts, analysts and observers—to compile a list of twenty cricketers who, they feel, would shape the world of cricket in the 2020s and beyond[95]. After analysing the birth charts of these twenty cricketers, I have selected five cricketers who will go on to become legends and superstars of the game.

I'm wary of the actual birthdates of cricketers from the Indian subcontinent. Many of them provide incorrect ages, while some from Bangladesh and Pakistan don't even know their exact date of birth. Hopefully, the birth details in this list are real.

Cricketers who will become superstars of the game:

Noor Ahmad

What a horoscope! This Afghanistan left-arm spinner has all the makings of a legend. Noor was born with a unique set of planets. As a result, he will end up playing both franchise and international cricket successfully. Noor's hero is Rashid Khan, and he can emulate him and probably even outshine him. Planet-X, Uranus, Pluto, Planet-Z, Planet-Y—he has so many planets in strong positions! His longevity in the game and success is assured.

Naseem Shah

It is extraordinary how Pakistan produces high-quality fast bowlers continuously. Naseem Shah made his test debut in November 2019, which coincided with the entry of Pluto into exaltation after almost seventy years. This classical right-arm fast bowler with an impressive pace and accuracy has an unusual horoscope. He has as many as eight planets in strong positions and promising debut date. Naseem will terrorise batsmen for many years and will be a great match-winner for his country.

---

[95]   '20 Cricketers for the 2020s', *The Cricket Monthly*, 20 June 2020, https://www.thecricketmonthly.com/story/1224850/20-cricketers-for-the-2020s.

Akbar Ali

Akbar Ali came into the limelight with an unbeaten 43 runs in the 2020 Under-19 World Cup final match. The first World Cup win for Bangladesh in any format, this innings was an indicator that the wicket-keeper–batsman is here to stay. Ali has Planet-X in deep exaltation and Chiron and Planet-Z in nascent exaltation, indicating something special about him. This Bangladeshi cricketer will play a role in taking the sport to the next level in his country.

Ibrahim Zadran

Ibrahim will be one of the best players ever produced by Afghanistan. He is likely to go a long way in world cricket. When Ibrahim was born, Planet-X just got into deep exaltation in Aquarius, the best zodiac sign for the planet phenomenally. An intensely passionate cricketer, he will give his hundred per cent on the cricket field. Afghanistan can always expect a miracle and a chance for victory as long as he is on the field. His never-say-die attitude will bring him many admirers across the world.

Rahmanullah Gurbaz

This boy is fearless and skilled too! He has an excellent chart with many planets in just the right positions. The boy, born with a deeply exalted Planet-X, will also become one of the superstars of Afghanistan. He comes from a difficult background will go on to script extraordinary, heroic stories. Rahmanullah will perform some outstanding Houdini acts, which will be awe-inspiring. He will be a superstar for many franchises. His treatment of veteran international bowlers and his will to win matches will earn him many ardent fans across the globe.

The horoscopes of Ibrahim, Noor Mohammad, Rahmanullah Gurbaz and the veteran Rashid Khan reiterate that Afghanistan will soon take huge strides in world cricket. Some Afghan players are already making waves in franchise cricket. It seems that even their national cricket will get a boost with young, fantastic players on the ground. Something really big is on the anvil for Afghanistan cricket.

Prediction #49
Samit and Anvay Dravid

How many great sportsmen have children who went on to become exceptional players in the same game? We may eventually witness something of this sort in India. The unassuming cricket legend Rahul Dravid's sons will play for the country and achieve success.

Interestingly, both have different styles. While the elder son, Samit, is a classical, orthodox player like his father, the younger one, Anvay, is the opposite. He believes in assaulting the opposition using brute power, and taking risks.

Samit is a combination of the technically correct Virgo, the pleasing-to-the-eye, Libra, with the infectious energy of Sagittarius. Don't be surprised if he reminds you of his father, while he plays those glorious cover drives. Samit will build his innings slowly and steadily and will be the backbone of any team. He has an extraordinary horoscope with six planets in strong positions. He is going to be a great run-getter, with the moniker 'run machine' attached to him, and will easily be a rich and famous cricketer.

Planet-X, in his horoscope, is in the deepest exaltation in its rarest avatar in Aquarius, a la Amitabh Bachchan or Muhammad Ali. Samit will ensure he plays some exceptional knocks for the country that even his father will be proud of. He even has the potential to be the captain.

Anvay, on the other hand, could either open the batting, destroy the opposition, and help his team set a target, or come down later in the order and finish off the game with unusual calmness and maturity of the Taurus in him. His

Planet-X, too, is deeply exalted, in the mould of an Arnold Schwarzenegger or a Franz Beckenbauer. He also has Venus and Mars in conjunction, an extremely desirable arrangement for sportspeople who use brute force. Cristiano Ronaldo, Bruce Lee, Lin Dan, Mike Tyson, all have this combination, which will make Anvay a dangerous and explosive batsman. Most of his runs will come when his team is in dire straits. He will play some extraordinary knocks and pull his team out of the woods. His icy-cool temperament will be an asset to the teams for which he plays.

Looking at the strength of the planets, I'm tempted to use more adjectives and compare the two with some big names in cricket, but I'll restrain myself so that there is no undue pressure on the duo. But the happy news is that Indian cricket seems to be in good hands with these two around.

Prediction #50
What Should the IPL Teams Do to Win an IPL Title?

Based on my study of IPL over a dozen years, I would say that there are three parameters for an IPL win.

A captain born in the right year
An astrologically well-balanced squad
A coach with a fantastic chart

The year of a captain's birth is significant. The logical progression depends on the placement of the higher planets, in the hierarchy, in strong positions. In recent times the winning captains in different sports have been born in 1981, 1983, 1986, 1987, 1990—1994. M.S. Dhoni and Gautam Gambhir were born in 1981. Rohit Sharma was born in 1987, and the future great captains would be those born in the early 1990s. That is the logical progression. Uranus and Neptune were the strongest planets during 1981–1987, and Neptune and Pluto were the strongest in the 1990s.

The legends of IPL, M.S. Dhoni, Gautam Gambhir and Rohit Sharma, who have won at least a couple of IPL titles, have fantastic horoscopes with a strong seventh house. The winning captain needs to have Uranus, Neptune, Pluto or Planet-X either exalted or in their own house—in the seventh—or one of them should be his seventh lord and exalted. In astrological terms, 'well-balanced' means having players born during the years when the planets higher in the hierarchy were in strong positions.

Mumbai Indians

They are sitting pretty with probably the best captain of the decade—Rohit Sharma. They are also lucky that a few team members are fantastic potential replacements for Rohit whenever he decides to call it a day. The 1993-born Hardik Pandya has all the makings of a successful captain. Mumbai Indians (MI) needn't worry till 2023–2024, till Rohit's charm is working. Even post-Rohit, MI would require minimal adjustments to have a super-strong, successful team in place. They have already won a few tournaments with Mahela Jayawardena as the coach. A new coach would add better strength to the team.

Royal Challengers Bangalore

The Royal Challengers (RCB) haven't won an IPL yet, which is a huge surprise. They will eventually win one, with Virat Kohli's superb horoscope. It is interesting how the RCB has continuously been making major mistakes during the auctions. Most of the time, they have ended up with incompetent players, leaving the team vulnerable. They haven't had a proper astrological balance in their squad, which has created all the problems. From the next IPL, they need to discard all the players born in the 1980s to enhance their chances to win an IPL. A.B. de Villiers who has a phenomenally exceptional chart, is the only exception. Simon Katich the head coach has it in him to win a tournament or two.

Chennai Super Kings

Chennai Super Kings (CSK) will be in an awkward situation without a leader after Dhoni plays his last IPL in 2021. 'Chinna thala' which means the second leader in command, 1986-born Suresh Raina, is the only able successor, but the karmic quota for the 1986-87-borns is almost over now. CSK needs a long-term replacement, and they don't have a capable young man in his twenties to replace Dhonilling, leaving a huge vacuum. If CSK doesn't acquire a 1990–1994-born strong player from the other teams in the upcoming auctions, they are looking at some barren seasons ahead. They also need to change the coach, Stephen Fleming. There is a limit to the number of wins a coach can deliver, too.

Delhi Capitals

Wow, what a team! Shreyas Iyer, the 1994-born charismatic young leader, has a superb horoscope, good enough to bag him a few IPL wins and make him a legend. He has some of the best younger players of the tournament with fantastic horoscopes at his disposal. With many years of play ahead of them and their karmic quotas still intact, this team is fail-proof. With a strong Jupiter, the legendary Ricky Ponting adds to the team's muscle as its coach. To win, they just need to offload a few older members, born in the 1980s, and get some new younger ones.

Rajasthan Royals

In recent years, no other team has, time and again, made the blunder of having fantastic players but being an astrological disaster. For starters, Ben Stokes's horoscope indicates great successes after overcoming extraordinary adversaries. Those chances are higher as a finisher; but they wasted him as an opener. Also, their choice of captain has been really baffling. They have Jos Buttler with an incredible horoscope and the right birth year to win an IPL (he is a 1990-born). Instead, they made Sanju Samson, a 1994-born, as the captain. Sanju has a good horoscope, but he is the future. Someone born in 1990-93 has better chances at winning than initially. Also, Shreyas, with his incredible horoscope, is more likely to succeed than another 1994-born. Unless RR get their playing XI right, they will find it difficult to win an IPL. The lack of a designated coach also impacts their chances.

Kolkata Knight Riders

Eoin Morgan was appointed the captain on an amavasya (moonless) day in 2020, midway through the tournament. The day signified that Morgan's tenure with KKR would be turbulent. Being a 1986-born, he does have it in him to win at least one more major title, besides the World Cup he won for England. KKR can bet on that possibility, but not for long. But, after that, the team doesn't have a capable young leader to take over. Shubman Gill would be too young to win an IPL as the natural progression of the planets will take many years for a 1999-born to win a tournament. They clearly don't have a number two in the team who can replace Morgan. In the next auction, they need to hire some young talents born in the early to mid-1990s to be groomed for future leadership. Brendon McCullum has loads of karmic quota left to win a major tournament, as a coach.

Sunrisers Hyderabad

This team is known to hire the best resources at lowest prices. They really have a solid, astrologically well-balanced core. They made captain David Warner step down and replaced him with Kane Williamson, a 1990-born. This is a brilliant move and dramatically increases their chances to win an IPL. The team is otherwise perfect astrologically and will punch above their weight, as they always do. Trevor Bayliss is a veteran in winning major tournaments, and his karmic quota is a bit doubtful. A coach born in the 1970s would have better chances to win for the SRH.

Punjab Kings

This brilliantly balanced team is ready to win tournaments under K.L. Rahul, the Indian player who has the best horoscope after Virat Kohli and Rohit Sharma. That he is very young and can remain the captain for a long time will strengthen the side. The squad, too, is astrologically well-balanced. They have a great coach—Anil Kumble—with an extraordinary horoscope and a remaining karmic quota. Besides, there could have been no better moment to rename the team as Punjab Kings in 2021, when Neptune and Pluto were in the strongest positions. This team's time has come.

Prediction #51

Is There Something More to Rafa than Meets the Eye?

There are passionate Rafael Nadal fans, and they naturally hate Roger Federer, and vice versa. 'Who is the greatest' is a never-ending discussion, and this prediction isn't about that, or how many Grand Slams will each one end up with.

The extraordinary difference in the playing style of the two star players can be attributed to their Moon signs, which are exactly the opposite. Nadal has his Moon in Aries, and Federer has it in Libra. While Libra is all about style, finesse and smoothness, Aries is all about aggression, passion and going all out. While Libra is easy on the eye, watching an Aries will wear you out sitting in your living room. It isn't humanly possible to keep playing the way Nadal does, and it will undoubtedly have repercussions.

Nadal has now admitted that his playing style has taken a toll on his health[96]. An Aries wants to win and win at all costs, so he keeps pushing himself harder and harder, sometimes beyond his body's capacity. He has been on painkillers almost

---

[96] Rafael Nadal Admits "Physical Issues" Have Taken Their Toll on Him but He's Happy to Still Be on Top', *tennishead*, 14 January 2020, https://tennishead.net/rafael-nadal-admits-physical-issues-have-taken-their-toll-on-him-but-hes-happy-to-still-be-on-top/.

throughout his career, since he started winning Grand Slams in 2005. The obvious areas of vulnerability have led to leg, knee and back problems. But the planets show that there is possibly more to it than meets the eye.

Planet Pluto is in deep debilitation in the Grey Lizard avatar in his ascendant, the first house of the body. This clearly shows the wear and tear of body parts. Chiron, his tenth lord is debilitated in the eighth house, which indicates the injuries he has picked up during his playing career. But the more serious problem is that Nadal also has Planet-X, the eighth lord of chronic health issues, in debilitation, in his eleventh house—of the second half of life. This indicates serious repercussions to his health in his forties to the sixties.

The first house indicates the body, the eighth house indicates serious health adversities, and the eleventh house indicates the second half of life. And, in Rafa's case, all of them are interlinked in a not-very-nice way. The worrying news is that they may not be indicators of sports injuries alone. He could face health complications on other fronts, too. The root cause of many of them may stem from his particularly intense style of playing but needn't necessarily happen during his playing days. Rafa needs to acknowledge and address these issues before it is too late. So, the worry is actually not about the immediate but what follows.

Prediction #52
What Should LeBron James Be Careful About?

LeBron James, the professional American basketball player, has an extraordinary horoscope that catapults him into the highest category of athletes but, at the same time, can also give him some extraordinary sufferings and troubles in life. The sufferings and troubles are yet to come.

Neptune in exaltation in the seventh house of enemies or competitors makes the Olympic gold medallist one of the greatest basketball players ever. The Lakers superstar also has Venus and Mars in conjunction, making him an explosive ball of energy and one of the greatest forwards in basketball.

The Jupite-Neptune conjunction in the seventh house makes him one of the most decorated players with the highest titles. James has been a world champion, and the winner of the biggest tournaments because of this position. The exalted Uranus in the sixth house also makes him a great athlete. In short, he is the Michael Phelps or the M.S. Dhoni of basketball, as both these great players share the same Gemini ascendant and the same set of planets in the same positions.

LeBron James also has a planetary position very similar to Michael Phelps. He has a debilitated Planet-X in the third house, and also Pluto, the sixth lord, debilitated in the fifth house. Michael Phelps went through a few psychological impediments when he was young. He faces dyslexia and ADH[97]. He even went through suicidal thoughts and depression, despite being the greatest Olympic medal winner ever[98]. LeBron James, too, has exactly the same planetary positions. He has managed to escape their impact for so long—unless he hasn't let us know. But he may not be able to avoid the troubles for very long in the future.

James's problems are not only about the mind but also the body. Pluto, the sixth lord of health, has got debilitated in his eighth house, of chronic health issues, from 2020. Even Planet-X will enter his first house in 2022. Planet-X is his twelfth lord of deep-rooted psychological problems and losses. It doesn't auger well entering into his first house of the body. LeBron James may go through some life-altering physical and

[97] 'Celebrity Spotlight: How Michael Phelps' ADHD Helped Him Make Olympic History', *Understood*, https://www.understood.org/en/learning-thinking-differences/personal-stories/famous-people/celebrity-spotlight-how-michael-phelps-adhd-helped-him-make-olympic-history, accessed 15 March 2021.

[98] Adam Wells, 'Michael Phelps Says He Contemplated Suicide, Struggled with Depression', *B/R*, 19 January 2018, https://bleacherreport.com/articles/2754933-michael-phelps-says-he-contemplated-suicide-struggled-with-depression.

psychological troubles over the next decade. These could be linked. Lebron

Prediction #53
SRK/SK/AK/AK--What's Next?

Just one combined chapter on Shah Rukh, Salman, Aamir and Akshay?

Enough has been written about them already. They are living legends; I can write nothing dramatically different. I wish I could have predicted something about them twenty-five years earlier.

By the way, amongst these four, who do you think has the best horoscope? By 'best', I mean whose horoscope ensures greater prosperity, longevity in the industry, and fewer troubles in personal and professional lives?

That undoubtedly is Akshay Kumar. Akshay has only two planets in debilitation—Planet-Y and Chiron. Both are placed in his fifth house, generally connected with love and romance, and indicate the problems in his personal relationships. Barring that, he has a phenomenal horoscope. It is an astrologer's dream, with the top five planets—Jupiter, Saturn, Uranus, Neptune and Pluto—all, yes, all of them, in exaltation! And, they are exalted in the right places. He is going to remain popular for a long time to come. He is going to do more movies and make a lot of money. His son Aarav, too, will join the industry and take his legacy forward. The smart investor that Akshay is, he will keep increasing his wealth. The good thing about Akshay's horoscope is that he will court fewer controversies and troubles in the latter part of his life.

Shah Rukh Khan probably has the best horoscope amongst all, in terms of achievements in the film industry. He has the planets Neptune, Pluto, Chiron and Planet-X, in 25 degrees, indicating that he will remain the biggest legend of all. He will be remembered and revered for long. His international popularity will continue to soar. The transit of exalted Pluto, his second lord, into his fourth house shows that he will continue to acquire great wealth over a period of time, into the 2020s and 2030s. SRK will add more businesses to his portfolio and become a business tycoon, too—an industry by himself. However, Planet-Y is debilitated in his sixth house of health, and he needs to mind his health, which seems to be the weak link in his horoscope.

Believe it or not, Aamir Khan is not a perfectionist. He is not a Virgo, he is a Piscean. Aamir Khan is all heart. He has made movies because he loves them, and not because they bring him money. He will continue to do what he does best—making wonderful movies without overthinking about the outcome. He will win some and lose some, but will leave an enduring legacy. Aamir will be connected to movies till his last breath as that is the only thing he knows and wants to know. Azad Rao Khan, the youngest child of Aamir has a brilliant horoscope and it does seem Aamir Khan's legacy will continue to thrive vibrantly.

I know there is only one question people want to ask about Salman Khan. When will he get married? My response is—does he need to? Ironically, one of the sexiest men alive has all the planets connected to marriage, love, romance and marital life in the weakest positions. His Venus and Mars are in conjunction in the twelfth house, indicating the struggles he has had in his previous relationships. His seventh lord, Planet-Z, is debilitated in the fifth house, which is why he has not married so far. Even right now, Planet-Z is debilitated, and will remain so till 2025. Then, during 2026–2033, Planet-Z will come into his seventh house. This means that even if he gets married, his marital life will not be very smooth.

I've noticed one strange thing in his chart. Planet-X, his fourth lord, will get exalted in his fifth house in 2022 and remain exalted beyond that. The fourth and fifth houses indicate children. What does Salman Khan have to do with children? Again, it's the same question I wondered about when I looked at Karan Johar's horoscope. I will not make the same mistake again. Therefore, if Salman Khan goes on to have a child, don't be too surprised. And he need not necessarily be married for that.

Prediction #54

Ranveer vs Varun: Who Will Inch Ahead?

Both Ranveer Singh and Varun Dhawan are lovable, talented young men, and we want both of them to succeed. But this subject has made it here, since it was requested by some enthusiasts.

Interestingly both Varun and Ranveer were born with the same ascendant, Virgo. Ranveer and Varun have their seventh lord, Neptune, in exaltation, making them the popular film actors they are. Both also have Uranus in exaltation in their third house, indicating control over their voice and communication skills. Both are great mimics; both have sung for their movies. Both are also passionate about film-making. Don't be surprised if either or both of them direct a movie too.

Coming to the transits, Neptune will come into its own house—the seventh house of art and public influence, in 2021, and stay there for fourteen years, until 2036. Uranus, too, will be exalted in the tenth house, of career, during 2031–2037, showing that these two actors are here to stay, and will continue to do well in their careers, probably peaking in the 2030s.

The biggest hurdle for the two will be the transit of Pluto into their fifth house. The fifth house indicates name, fame, popularity and children, and both of them could get sucked into one of the negative manifestations of Pluto. They need to be careful about their words and actions, for they could lead to defamation or ignominy in some way. Something connected to children could also be a botheration for them. Both have Chiron debilitated in the ninth house, indicating that they need to be careful about law and legal matters.

Now, let us come to the differences between the two. Planet-X is strongly placed in the ascendant for Varun Dhawan, indicating a more or less stable career. Ranveer Singh has Planet-X in debilitation in the twelfth house of losses, sounding a warning regarding his investments. His wife Deepika's horoscope also indicates that both need to be careful about leaky buckets through which money could flow away.

The biggest differentiating factor between Ranveer and Varun is Pluto. Both have it debilitated, but Ranveer has it in the Grey Lizard avatar. At times, he tends to go a bit overboard in his enthusiasm, and he needs to learn to control that. Pluto is his third lord, and he may say or do certain things which could be held against him and could even lead to a loss of reputation. He has been embroiled in smaller controversies earlier, like the AIB roast in 2015[99]. Pluto is now in a stronger avatar, and he may find himself in bigger controversies, which could even threaten to derail his career.

Who will inch ahead if we assume there is a race? Unquestionably Varun! He has more planets in stronger positions, and in deeper exaltation, as compared to Ranveer. And yes, Varun wouldn't commit the kind of hara-kiri which the living-on-the-edge Ranveer can—he always courts that extra trouble.

Prediction #55
How Far Can Tiger Shroff Go?

When I wrote in 2014 that Tiger Shroff would become a superstar, many people were surprised[100]. Often, an alternative narrative is spun around promising young actors, in the intensely competitive Indian Hindi film industry. I remember the nasty

[99] 'A Complete Timeline of AIB Knockout: Who Said What', *Hindustan Times*, 17 February 2015, https://www.hindustantimes.com/entertainment/a-complete-timeline-of-aib-knockout-who-said-what/story-qgTgpKcpp4JWK4lBQfqLeM.html.

[100] 'What! This Astrologer Had Predicted Tiger Shroff's Bollywood Success in 2014', *India TV*, 2 April 2018, https://www.indiatvnews.com/entertainment/bollywood-tiger-shroff-bollywood-success-in-2014-astrologer-prediction-baaghi-2-actor-435541.

comments over Shroff's looks and the memes. Tiger Shroff not just overcame the criticism and the agenda against him but delivered the hit movie, *Baaghi*. But the sceptics still wouldn't accept his success.

A leading film producer once asked me if Tiger could deliver big. I said yes. Unfortunately, the producer only implemented half of what I had recommended. Despite my repeated reiterations, they did not realise that while an actor's birth chart may be powerful, other factors like the director and the producer's horoscopes also matter in the success of a movie. They signed Tiger immediately, but they also hired a director with a weak horoscope. The movie was a failure.

The question that remained was, could Tiger Shroff still become a superstar as I had predicted? Well, the answer was a resounding 'yes'. After 2018, Tiger was already way ahead of his contemporaries[101]. Tiger is evolving as a reliable bet. He is already an established star.

From 2021 onwards, his success will only go north. Pluto had just entered its own house when Tiger was born—after 256 years. Tiger was born a few weeks after Sachin Tendulkar made his debut for India. The planets influencing him are the same. It is a powerful nascent Pluto, indeed.

Pluto, in the eleventh house in his birth chart, indicates success as he grows older. Tiger also has a powerful Planet-X, @responsible for him being an actor. He also has a very strong Planet-Z, which is responsible for his physique, athletic attributes, status as a sex symbol, and all the daredevilry he performs on the screen.

The exalted Neptune in Tiger Shroff's twelfth house makes him a fabulous dancer and an acrobat. Neptune and Pluto will be favourable in the future too. The eleventh lord Pluto will be exalted in his first house, ensuring success for the next twenty

[101] Popdiaries, 'This Is How Tiger Shroff Beats His Contemporaries Arjun-Varun!', *Yahoo!Style*, 25 July 2018, https://in.style.yahoo.com/tiger-shroff-beats-contemporaries-arjun-093212281.html.

years. Tiger Shroff will not just be a commercially successful actor, but also a successful producer. His projects will turn out to be huge successes financially. Neptune can give him international collaborations, and this will only get bigger and better. He can also mastermind some creative ventures, which will turn out to be successful businesses. Tiger Shroff's success story will continue from 2021 to 2041, and even beyond.

Prediction #56

All Is Not Well with Saifeena.

Kareena Kapoor has a brilliant horoscope with extraordinary possibilities in her life. At the same time, she also has some planets whose manifestations could be highly problematic for her in the future.

Kareena's tenth lord Chiron, exalted in her seventh house, is the foundation of her showbiz career. And Uranus, the fifth lord, got into nascent exaltation in the second house, making her the number one actress in the industry during the peak of her career.

Kareena will shift her focus to family in the next decade. This is indicative of a positive Pluto's transition into her fourth house in 2020. It will stay there till 2040, so we will be seeing less of Kareena in films soon. But she may make a comeback with some interesting roles in the 2030s.

While her positive planets have made her what she is, a few weak planets haven't manifested themselves yet. Kareena's sixth lord of health, Neptune, is very weakly placed. Planet-X, her eighth lord, is in debilitation in her eleventh house. The weakness of her eighth house of chronic ailments is adding to Neptune's impact. It shows that Kareena can be afflicted by health challenges. The eleventh lord Planet-Z being debilitated indicates that this will happen in the second half of her life. It's worrying that these positions are similar to Michael Jackson and Sridevi.

Kareena Kapoor has five planets in the twelfth house, which is also a worry. The twelfth is a strange house. Connections to foreign countries is a positive manifestation; else, it can indicate losses. Unlike Madhuri Dixit or Irrfan Khan, Kareena doesn't seem to have an international connection. Therefore the congregation of planets in the twelfth means huge losses. These weak planets could indicate hurdles in the area of finance or business ventures. She may enter some business ventures, which could lead to losses or the disappearance of a source of income due to unforeseen reasons. The planets in the twelfth house also indicate mental and emotional stress, so Kareena needs to be emotionally strong.

The fourth lord Planet-Y is also transiting into Kareena's husband Saif Ali Khan's sixth house, indicating health concerns for a family member. In addition, Pluto is his sixth lord and is transiting into his eighth house, indicating problems pertaining to his health and longevity too.

It does seem that Saifeena may have to brace themselves for some tough times ahead.

Prediction #57
The Life of Priyanka Chopra

Priyanka Chopra surely has an extraordinary arrangement of planets, but she also has some karmic remnants she needs to take care of. In fact, her model horoscope can even be used to explain astrological terms. Neptune in nascent exaltation in her eighth house makes her a model and a Miss World. Planet-Y, the fifth lord, is deeply exalted, making her a film star and a singer. And the tenth lord, Uranus, in deep exaltation in her seventh house, makes her a superstar.

At the same time, some planets are placed in the weakest positions. Priyanka has her ascendant lord Planet-X in debilitation in her fourth house. The fourth lord, Planet-Z, is in debilitation in the fifth house. Even her ninth lord, Saturn, is in debilitation in the fifth house, which stands for love, romance and children. The fourth house too indicates children. Many women, who have debilitated planets in the fourth and fifth houses, have gynaecological problems or issues with either childbearing or their children.

Most importantly, her seventh lord Pluto is the weakest planet in her chart. It is in nascent debilitation. The seventh house indicates marriage, and she had a high-profile wedding. Pluto, her seventh lord, will be traversing her ninth house, of foreign countries, in the next decade. That shows why she is married to Nick Jonas, a foreigner. But, more importantly, Pluto is in debilitation, which implies that everything connected with love, romance and foreign travel will not be easy for her. Pluto indicates that marriage could be the biggest challenge of her life.

The minor problem could be that she, or her husband, would have to keep shuttling between countries, which could strain their relationship. And as the planet involved here is Pluto, there could even be a larger problem in the relationship.

A look into Nick Jonas's horoscope reveals chances of more than one strong relationship; sometimes, it could even mean more than one marriage. Jonas has Saturn in the seventh house, which indicates a spouse with a considerable age difference. His Mars is in the twelfth house, making him a manglik. His Venus, too, is in a weak position, indicating that the woman in his life will go through some suffering. Sometimes this can also indicate a strong relationship after a marriage has ended. Nick has been in a few relationships earlier, but this is his first marriage. He also has a weak planet in the fifth house of children, which could also be a cause for concern.

The challenging time in Priyanka and Nick's life would be from 2025 to 2030. This is the time when Chiron, Priyanka's third house of the mind, will be debilitated in her twelfth house of foreign countries and Planet-Z will come into her fourth house of family. Everything connected with her family, home, and children will lead to huge mental and emotional trauma during this phase. Looking at the fact that Pluto too is involved, it does look like she will be able to hold on to things for long.

Prediction #58

What Lies Ahead for Deepika Padukone?

Deepika Padukone was born in Copenhagen, Denmark, and that is a huge blessing in disguise for her. Her horoscope shows Planet-X in nascent exaltation in her twelfth house of foreign countries. It indicates that her success could have come only in a foreign country. India is technically a foreign country for her, and that works well for her. Her fifth lord, Uranus, is exalted, making her a film star, and her Planet-Z is in deep exaltation in the ascendant, which makes her a beautiful style icon, and accords her a strong association with the glamour world.

Deepika has had a fantastic career so far, and she is presently the reigning queen of Bollywood. She will eventually relinquish the position of number one to a younger woman born in the 1990s. But irrespective of that, Deepika will remain relevant for several years. Uranus, her fifth lord of fame and popularity, will remain exalted till 2024 in her seventh house. She will get great projects as an actor till then. Post 2024, the planet will be debilitated, signifying that she will move away from the limelight.

Uranus will come back into exaltation from 2031 to 2037 once again, although into her ninth house this time. Post 2031 too, Uranus could put her behind the camera or explore other branches of the media industry as the ninth house indicates a more behind-the-scenes role in the entertainment world. During 2025–2030, Planet-Z will move into her eleventh house, suggesting that she will enter other allied activities connected with the media world, more from a business perspective, if not as a lead actress. Uranus and Planet-Z will help maintain her association with the film world as a director or a producer. Neptune will remain in her sixth house of opportunities throughout the 2020s, and she will benefit from that.

A couple of things might bother her, though. Pluto, her second lord, will be debilitated in her fourth house of family, home, real estate and children. The second house means money and wealth. These are a few areas where she may face some inconveniences in the 2020s.

She might have to make frequent visits to a gynaecologist or face problems connected with children. Something related to her immediate family could also be a cause for concern. She also needs to check her real estate investments and be careful about some leaky bucket in terms of her financials.

Neptune going into her sixth house could cause some health irritants. Even in her birth chart, she has a debilitated Pluto in the ascendant, which warns of some physical problems. Or perhaps someone or something could malign her in some way. Deepika needs to be aware and careful.

The love and romance area looks promising, as Uranus will be transiting her seventh house. It seems everything will be great in Deepika and Ranveer Singh's love life. Now that is a big relief!

Prediction #59

What Lies Ahead for Kangana Ranaut?

Kangana Ranaut is a Leo–Aquarius–Pisces. She is very artistic, versatile, creative, generous and fearless. At the same time, she can also be headstrong, bordering on arrogant, extremely sensitive and a rebel.

Kangana, like all Leos and Aquarians, would want to do something big and impactful. Money is not the big motivator for a Leo–Aquarius–Pisces. She is undoubtedly not a schemer, nor is she sly or a cunning social climber. What motivates her is getting appreciation for her work, being respected and feeling meaningful. This combination of zodiac signs makes her call a spade a spade, without worrying about the consequences. Her third house is very weak with debilitated Planet-Y placed there; its lord Chiron too is debilitated. The third house indicates the tongue and the mind. She will face issues due to her acidic tongue and will go through some intense emotional challenges.

Kangana has been in the news for all the wrong reasons since the death of actor Sushant Singh Rajput. Sushant's death coincided with the entry of planet Pluto, Kangana's seventh lord, in the ninth house. Kangana has a negative Pluto, and she will face Pluto's negative impact because of this position. Pluto will stay here for a long time, which could spell significant problems for her.

Since Pluto is her seventh lord, its effects will reflect in Kangana's relationships, public acclaim, and her association with politics and the government. It is also why she has been antagonising many people on public platforms and creating many enemies publicly. The number of her enemies may go up in the future. In fact, she has already been facing problems with the Maharashtra government[102]. Pluto's seventh–ninth connection could also lead Kangana to legal complications.

Kangana is a manglik, which means she has Mars in the eighth house in her birth chart. She has had a lot of grief in her personal life already, and it seems it will continue. The weak seventh lord indicates that she may not find reprieve in her personal life, even in the coming decade. It won't be surprising if Kangana decides to stay single. If she chooses to get married, she could face a series of disappointments, leading to separation or divorce.

The positive aspect of Kangana's horoscope is the transit of the exalted Neptune into her eleventh house that indicates

[102] Saurabh Gupta, edited by Divyanshu Dutta Roy, 'Kangana Ranaut vs Maharashtra Government Over "Mumbai–PoK" Remark', *NDTV*, 4 September 2020, https://www.ndtv.com/india-news/kangana-ranaut-has-no-right-to-live-in-mumbai-if-she-feels-unsafe-maharashtra-minister-amid-row-over-her-remarks-2290453.

the second half of life. Meaning she will be around in films for some time. Kangana will continue to be relevant in her forties and fifties, but more in the background than the foreground as Uranus, her tenth lord of career, is entering her twelfth house of behind-the-scenes. The eleventh house indicates business profits. Some of Kangana's business ventures and productions connected with the media world should turn out to be profitable.

Prediction #60

Alia Bhatt: How Far Can She Go?

Looks can be deceptive, isn't it? When people saw Alia Bhatt for the first time in 2012, in *Student of the Year*, the general impression was that she'd be a one-movie wonder and would eventually fade away. At least, I thought so until I saw her horoscope. Her acting talent wasn't evident then. Since then, she has matured and proved her detractors wrong—and how! Alia's fantastic acting skills come from her Sun in Pisces, which gives her the chameleonic ability to get into the skin of any character. She is definitely more intelligent than she came across in *Koffee with Karan*, with her Mercury in the intelligent Aquarius. The Moon in Scorpio gives her the intensity and passion for her profession.

Alia's horoscope is very powerful. It shows that she is here to stay for a long time. Planet-X, her fifth lord in exaltation in the twelfth house, indicates that she will be a celebrated filmstar. Pluto in its own eleventh house will make her even more successful in her thirties and forties. Her Neptune will traverse her third house in the 2020s and 2030s. You can expect her to dabble in singing even more or become a writer or director and producer. Neptune, in its own twelfth house, could make her an internationally acclaimed film star.

While her career will go northwards, and her best is yet to come, her personal life could be a cause for concern. Her seventh lord, Chiron, will be debilitated in the 2030s, leading to disturbances in her marital life. Her Planet-Y is debilitated in the eighth, and her eighth lord, Planet-Z, is debilitated in the eleventh, indicating gynaecological issues or problems with her immune system, and other health matters, in the later part of her life.

Alia also needs to manage her finances well. A weak Uranus in the twelfth house could make her lose money due to poor financial planning and mismanagement of funds. She needs to be doubly careful if she enters film production or decides to invest her hard-earned money in some fancy projects. There could be a leaky bucket she needs to plug.

Alia needs better advice and mentoring from close friends, especially in the second half of her life. She may just fritter away much of what she has earned in the first half of her life. And we aren't talking only about finances here. A strong eleventh house is the silver lining, which indicates that she will come back strongly in the latter half of her life despite all the personal, financial and physical problems she is bound to face in the intervening period.

Prediction #61
What Do the Stars Say about Ranbir Kapoor's Marriage?

Ranbir's horoscope could be a classic case study for an astrologer who practices using the Indian methods for predictions. Ranbir has a weak seventh house. He is a manglik, and Mars or Mangal is in his seventh house of marriage. I don't accept the concept as it is. It needs modifications. But, I don't disagree with it. There is enough evidence about the problems people face in life because of the placement of Mars in their seventh house. Mars indicates relationships in the horoscope of a male, and Venus indicates the women in his life. Venus is in debilitation in Ranbir's fifth house. Both Venus and Mars, planets essential for happiness in relationship, are in weak positions in Ranbir's horoscope. Show his chart to any Indian astrologer without specifying that it belongs to the superstar. He will tell you that the person will go through huge trials and tribulations in his personal life.

While the seventh house indicates marital life, the fifth house indicates love and romance. Ranbir has Planet-Z in debilitation in the fifth house indicating huge troubles here too. But the question arises—hasn't Ranbir been through many troubled relationships already? Wouldn't these planets indicate them? He even asked for Deepika Padukone's forgiveness on a public stage, before the whole nation[103]. Aren't the problems already done and dusted?

Well, he needs to be wary of his seventh lord, Pluto. Pluto is in debilitation in his horoscope, and is the seventh lord of marriage. It became debilitated in 2020, and will remain so for two decades. This points to the bigger relationship issues yet to come. While a weak Venus indicates that the woman in his life, post-marriage, will go through many hardships, his weak Mars indicates that all will not be well in the marriage. Pluto indicates that the marriage will end in a divorce or separation, or the partners will have to live lifelong in an unhappy relationship. Ranbir also has weak fourth and fifth house that co-rule children. Ranbir is looking at a very tough personal life. Besides problems in his personal life, the seventh and the ninth house connection indicates some legal troubles. He could find himself caught in legal battles.

Ranbir has already been through many bad times in love and romance, and in his relationships. But these times are far from over. Alia and Ranbir would make a cute couple, but everything may not turn out hunky-dory as they may be hoping. Alia also has weak fourth, fifth and seventh houses, which corroborate this possibility. Alia's eighth lord Chiron too is debilitated in her eleventh house denoting that if it is not about the relationships, then there could be something more severe.

---

[103] Moviez Adda, 'Ranbir Says Sorry to Deepika for Cheating?' *YouTube*, 3 September 2012, https://www.youtube.com/watch?v=QoH9nUxnM-4.

Prediction #62

What Will Karan Johar Do?

When I looked at Karan's horoscope in 2016, I saw the transit of Planet-Y into his fourth house of children, and I ignored any possibility, thinking Karan Johar could have nothing to do with children. But he ended up with a set of twins in 2017. In 2019, when I saw his horoscope again, I saw Pluto transiting the eighth house of controversy and death. I resisted the temptation to text and warn him about the health of a family member that could be a cause for concern, or that he could be at the centre of a controversy. But the problem here was, what could I say? It isn't clear what exactly the event would be until it unfolds. You get some clues about the manifestation, but not the exact episode. The positive part is that it keeps the suspense going, and life continues to be interesting.

Karan Johar was at the centre of a storm after the suicide of actor Sushant Singh Rajput. Kangana Ranaut, the media, and a larger part of the population went after Karan Johar on charges of nepotism. Does that mean Karan Johar and his movies will lose their earlier popularity and he will slowly disappear from public eye? Well, it doesn't seem so, astrologically. Karan Johar is here to stay, and for a long time.

The transit of Pluto into Johar's eighth house played up the controversy. Amongst other things, the eighth house suggests being maligned. It is also the house of death. Karan was lucky that he didn't have to deal with the death of someone close. He was unlucky that the death of someone not-so-close gave him more grief than he could have ever imagined. The eighth house is also the house of transformation. Expect Karan Johar to come back in some sort of a transformed avatar. Possibly, he will be a bit subdued and a bit more down-to-earth.

The most important planet in the horoscope, Uranus, will remain exalted in his eleventh house, of profits, till 2024. That implies that his businesses will continue to flourish. Between 2025 and 2035, he will continue to grow, and even enhance his position in the industry. He has a power centre of Uranus and Pluto conjunction in his fourth house, and he will continue to be a force to reckon with. He will make several movies with star kids. The smart Taurus businessman in him knows that they come with a readymade star appeal, and he cashes in on them the right way. Some of the biggest future superstars, star kids who will rule the 2020s and 2030s, will be mentored by Karan Johar.

Karan Johar will also mentor and guide many youngsters, without a privileged background. He will be responsible for launching at least one superstar of the 2020s with no film background. He may, after all, redeem himself and produce a couple of superstars from nowhere. Karan will remain relevant even in his sixties and seventies as the grand old man of Indian cinema.

Prediction #63

Ekta Kapoor's Comeback

Nokia, Yahoo, Kodak, Blackberry, Polaroid—does that ring a bell? They were all pioneering companies but couldn't go too far as they failed to innovate. Ekta Kapoor may just become another such example if she doesn't evolve.

Ekta Kapoor discovered the formula for success in the telly-world, from the early 1990s to the mid-2000s, when remarkably young. She created an alternative line of telly stars. She ignored the criticism that her serials were regressive and created an empire by catering to the tastes of a large section of the middle-class Indians with a rigid patriarchal mindset. She even ventured into mainstream cinema with moderate success.

Covid-19 has modified the world of many people, and Ekta Kapoor is perhaps one of them. She has a strong Pluto and a weak Uranus in her horoscope. Now, that is a strange combination.

Pluto brings in something new, makes its children a pioneer of sorts, but Uranus is all about innovation. Ekta took the stories of the 1940s and 1950s and presented them in a new format, thus producing some pioneering content in the TV industry, which made the viewership or TRPs (Television Rating Points) soar high. For entertainment on TV, Ekta was the queen.

But from 2021, her main domain—the small screen—is under threat, as most people with access to the internet have switched off their television sets in favour of alternative streaming and OTT (Over-the-Top) platforms. Kapoor's ALT Balaji, a video-on-demand venture in this sphere, hasn't really taken off as expected. Uranus, her ninth lord, is in debilitation in the eleventh house of business profits right now, and will remain so till 2024. She may lose her market share to other players and may have to cut down on her businesses and expenses significantly.

Pluto transiting into her eighth house of transformation shows that she will face obstacles in the rapidly transforming television industry. Ekta Kapoor will be swept away by the waves of new developments. The lack of a strong Uranus has left her devoid of new ideas, and therein lies her predicament. The transiting Pluto, her sixth lord, is moving into the eighth house and could lead to a health scare either to her, or her family. All in all, the period from 2021 to 2024 will be very tough for her.

But the fiery Aries, and the resolute Taurus that she is, though she loves to call herself a Gemini, she will bounce back in her career after 2024. She will come up with new ideas and create a niche for herself in the entertainment world once again.

This new lease of life will come from a strong Chiron and Planet-Z entering strong positions during 2025–2030. After 2031, Ekta's Uranus will come into her first house of personality, and she may be bereft of new ideas and inable to compete in the changed new world. If she tries to build something new during this time, she will only go down further and become completely irrelevant.

Prediction #64
What Will Brad Pitt Do Now?

Brad Pitt's drop-dead good looks, and his much-publicised personal life, have overshadowed his skill and success as a two-times Academy awards-winner. His career, too, has taken a backseat as his ascendant lord, Pluto, has been debilitated since 2006. But not anymore.

In 2020, Pluto moved into his third house of communication and leadership. This could mean that Brad Pitt will continue with his political and humanitarian causes and champion the disadvantaged people[104]. He could also turn a director or a writer. Neptune will remain exalted in his fifth house for the next fifteen years. Like good wine, Pitt will get better with age, not only in terms of looks but also in his film career.

Not many people know about Brad's passion for architecture[105]. A strong Chiron and the transition of Planet-X into his eighth house will make him undertake some interesting ventures in the area of architecture and housing.

In personal life, Neptune is moving into Brad Pitt's fifth house of love and romance. His seventh lord of relationships, Planet-X, will be exalted, meaning he will find love once again. Brad will still be carousing in his sixties, and people's interest in his life won't be over just yet.

Prediction #65
What Can Angelina Jolie Look Forward to?

Theirs was the most talked-about romance of the 2000s. She was one half of the portmanteau, Brangelina, which made headlines. But the magic of their love ended, sadly, in a separation. Pluto is

---

[104] 'Bono, Brad Pitt Launch Campaign for Third-World Relief', *MTV*, 4 June 2005, http://www.mtv.com/news/1499708/bono-brad-pitt-launch-campaign-for-third-world-relief/.

[105] Richard Jinman, 'From Troy to Hove – Brad Pitt's New Career', *The Guardian*, 27 May 2005, https://www.theguardian.com/society/2005/may/27/urbandesign.arts.

the fifth lord of romance, in Angelina's horoscope, and she entered a relationship with Brad Pitt in the 2010s, when it had just got into debilitation. The relationship was destined to be doomed.

Angelina has already been through two divorces, and this will be her third. The romantic Taurus–Pisces that she is, it will be painful to be without a partner.

Pluto, the lord of romance in her chart, since 2020, is now exalted in her horoscope till 2037. This is a long period for love to blossom in her life once again. She will not only find love again, but also forge a significant relationship, even a marriage. Since Pluto is exalted, it could last longer this time. Will it be someone from her past? Well, that cannot be ruled out.

Pluto is Angelina Jolie's fifth lord, of showbiz, and it is getting exalted in her seventh house of public influence. Her fame, popularity and success as a film star will grow considerably in the coming decade. She will do some truly ground-breaking work in this period. Angelina has evolved as an actor over the years and she has good reasons to look forward to the next two decades of her life.

Prediction #66
What›s in Store for George Clooney?

George Clooney is a favourite among women. He has topped almost all the charts based on looks, sartorial elegance, sense of style and sex appeal. He has won Academy Awards as both the lead actor and a supporting actor, highlighting his talent. His horoscope shows exciting times ahead for him in the 2020s.

Pluto, his tenth lord of career, is exalted in his seventh house; and the seventh lord, Planet-Z, is deeply exalted, making him a famous film star. Neptune is exalted in his ninth house, making him a successful director, producer and screenwriter. Clooney has been there, done that. In the future, Clooney's Neptune will transit in his second house, continuing his journey as a producer. Planet-X will get exalted in his fifth house, which shows that his stint as an actor is not over yet. This journey, too, shall continue.

The most interesting part of his future is that his career planet, the tenth lord, Pluto, will get exalted in the twelfth house that indicates foreign countries and philanthropy. The actor-activist-philanthropist will continue to impact lives positively, working for causes across the globe. In 2010, he helped collect donations for the Haiti earthquake victims, donated to charities in Lebanon[106] and advocated a resolution for the Darfur conflict. He has also been involved in charitable activities involving Syria, Armenia, and Brunei[107].

Besides organising rallies for fund-raising, Clooney will also donate large sums from his wealth.

But all may not necessarily be fine for the handsome superstar. Alas, George Clooney is a Grey Lizard, with Pluto in exaltation in 12 degrees. This could mean two things. As the transiting Pluto will be in the twelfth house, he may face massive opposition and impediments while executing his global causes. Sometimes Pluto makes the Grey Lizards go through extraordinarily tough situations before achieving what they want, almost making it look heroic. Clooney could go through such hardships while he plays a real-life hero.

The other possibility is that he may lose much of what he has, under some unusually tough circumstances, since the twelfth house also shows losses. Some unforeseen events could trigger financial losses and career setbacks. However, considering Clooney's history, and his associations, it seems the first possibility is more likely. But, by the end of it all, the Grey

---

[106]   Sarah Young, 'Beirut Explosion: George and Amal Clooney Donate £76,000 to Lebanese Relief Charities', *The Independent*, 7 August 2020, https://www. independent.co.uk/life-style/beirut-explosion-george-amal-clooney-donate-lebanon-charities-a9659096.html.

[107]   'UN Gives Actor Clooney Peace Role', *BBC News*, 1 February 2008, http://news.bbc. co.uk/2/hi/entertainment/7220701.stm.

Lizard will certainly put its stamp on George Clooney's life, especially when it enters its own zone during 2025-2028.

Prediction # 67

What Will Happen to Johnny Depp?

Johnny Depp has been through it all—from a struggling actor to becoming one of the biggest and the most successful film stars in Hollywood. He has been divorced twice and separated from four partners. He has been accused of domestic abuse, alcoholism and addiction for much of his life. He has been bankrupt. When will the wheel of fortune turn for Johnny Depp? Will his life ever become better?

Depp's Pluto entered his fifth house of fame and popularity, in the 1990s, when he started achieving success in the movies. He reached the peak of his career during 2003–2011, after the movie *Pirates of the Caribbean* and its sequels did very well at the box office. However, he has seen a decline in his career post-2012. In 2020, he was replaced in the third part of the movie *Fantastic Beasts,* after being found guilty of domestic violence[108].

Pluto, his fifth lord of fame, name and popularity, was in the deepest debilitation during 2017–2020. He lost all that he had. His reputation has been in shambles, his finances are at their lowest, and no one wants to work with him now as there could be a public outcry against him every time his movie releases. This is due to his eighth lord, the debilitated Uranus, transiting his tenth house of career. This could be the lowest that Depp could ever fall since it cannot get worse than this. Anything that happens from now on, can only be positive.

Luckily for Depp, it seems like the stars have finally made up their mind to shine on him again. In 2021, his Pluto is

---

[108] Benjamin Lee, 'Johnny Depp Says He Has Been Asked to Resign from Fantastic Beasts Franchise', *The Guardian,* 6 November 2020, https://www.theguardian.com/film/2020/ nov/06/johnny-depp-fantastic-beasts-resign-franchise-statement.

getting exalted in his seventh house of public acclaim. Neptune is entering its own house, his ninth house of luck and the law. These favourable transits could enable Depp's comeback from the depths of despair. Some legal issues will turn in his favour, and he could have a 'jail-break',' quite literally.

He may not suddenly become a good boy, or be completely exonerated, but he will be able to garner enough support so that there isn't too much prejudice against his movies or boycott of his work. A wave of sympathy could ensure that his films do well at the box office, restoring his career and finances.

Johnny Depp could become a changed and sober man. Since Neptune is entering his ninth house, he could even turn to spirituality in some way. Life will give Johnny Depp another chance, and this time, he will not squander it away.

Prediction #68
What Will Trouble Leonardo DiCaprio Forever?

One of the most talented and good-looking actors in the world, Leonardo DiCaprio, unfortunately, still awaits his happily-ever-after life. He is yet to be married and hasn't stuck to a relationship for long. And now it seems relationships will lead to more pain for him.

DiCaprio's seventh house of marriage, contains a debilitated Chiron, and the seventh lord, Neptune, is debilitated. Added to this, Venus and Mars, too, are in conjunction. Sadly, none of the planets connected with marriage and relationships are well placed in his charts.

Besides, the weak Neptune will enter his seventh house in 2022, and stay there till 2036. If he gets married, it will become a troubled marriage that could lead to an undesirable end. Instead, it will be wise to stay single and be spared of the ills of a broken marriage forever. Regardless, the *Titanic* star will continue to court controversies regarding his relationships. The seventh house also indicates the law, and there could even be some long-drawn legal fights and entanglements.

What would improve, though, is Leonardo DiCaprio's career. Pluto will be exalted in his fifth house for a long time, pushing his showbiz career to climb higher peaks. Since Pluto is DiCaprio's third lord, it won't be surprising if he becomes a director or a writer. At least one significant part of his life, his career, will continue to be fantastic for quite a while.

Prediction #69

What Else Will Jennifer Aniston Achieve?

I have some great news and some not-so-great news for Jennifer.

Amongst the top four planets, Uranus, Planet-X and Pluto are in deep exaltation in her horoscope. Uranus, the fifth lord, deeply exalted in the twelfth house, made her an internationally famous TV and film star. It led her to portray Rachel Green in the sitcom *Friends*, a character that is regarded as one of the most notable female characters in American television history[109]. Combined with Planet-X, her eighth lord, in exaltation in the ninth house, had her as a fixture on several lists for the world's greatest women.

Jennifer Aniston is a Scorpio–Capricorn. She yearns for stability in her family life. At the same time, she is a sharp businessperson behind a beautiful face. Jennifer's second lord, Pluto, is exalted in the eleventh house, indicating the potential to convert ideas into wealth. She is already a producer, and creates media content for streaming services. She has already co-founded and sold the shares of one of her companies to Unilever for an undisclosed amount, and has been a part of a couple of film production houses[110].

---

[109] Kim Potts, '100 Most Memorable Female TV Characters', *AOL TV*, 14 November 2014.

[110] Michael Fleming, 'Jennifer Aniston forms Echo Films, *Variety*, 31 March 2008, https://variety.com/2008/film/features/jennifer-aniston-forms-echo-films-1117983220/.

Pluto, Jennifer's second lord, is exalted in her fourth house. Her Uranus will remain exalted in her seventh house till 2024, and then during 2031–2039 in the ninth house. She will do incredibly well in the next two decades as well. Her financial worth will soar, as an actor-producer and creator. She will use her celebrity status smartly and, with some exciting business ideas in the entertainment industry, she will create valuable products.

Pluto is exalted in her fourth house, indicating stability in her family life, which is different from love and romance. Love will continue to be a painful area, as Chiron will remain debilitated in her seventh house during 2026–2032. However, she will make peace with most problems and manage a good family life in her fifties, sixties and beyond. Jennifer could even shift to a new home—to a bigger and better one in the mid 2020s.

The weakest planet in her horoscope, a debilitated Neptune, will transit into her sixth house in 2021, and remain there till 2036. This is the period when Aniston will hit her lowest in terms of her health. She was dyslexic in her pre-teens[111], and has been through some trauma and struggles, but this one will be a much bigger health challenge. Jennifer is a strong woman, and she will need to bring all her courage to the forefront to take care of this malaise, and she will do so admirably.

Prediction #70

What's Next for Beyoncé?

Beyoncé has an unbelievable horoscope, with Uranus, Chiron, Planet-Y, Planet-Z and Jupiter in exaltation, making her achieve glory and success. She is the most nominated woman at the Grammy Awards, and the highest-earning black musician in

---

[111] Stephen Galloway, 'Jennifer Aniston Reveals Struggles with Dyslexia, Anger; Shrugs Off Oscar Snub', *The Hollywood Reporter*, 21 January 2015, https://www. hollywoodreporter. com/news/jennifer-aniston-reveals-struggles-dyslexia-764854.

history[112]. Beyoncé and her husband, rapper and businessman Jay-Z, make one of the most powerful couples in the world[113].

Unfortunately, she has just stepped into one of the most testing phases of her life. From 2021, debilitated Neptune will transit Beyoncé's seventh house of marriage and partnerships. She also has both Venus and Mars, the planets responsible for marital happiness, in debilitation. This puts her relationship with Jay-Z under a cloud. The couple will enter a very troubled phase in their relationship in the 2020s, and this may eventually lead to a breakup, both in their personal life and in the businesses partnership.

Supposing the relationship stays strong, then there could be another problem. Jay-Z might go through some troubles financially or physically, which would impact Beyoncé significantly. The seventh house can also indicate some legal issues or partnership troubles. Beyoncé may face some large losses in her life, either material or emotional, in the 2020s, and that would have a lot to do with her spouse. Beyonce and Jay-Z are looking at some seriously tough times ahead.

Prediction #71
What Will Kanye West Do Now?

Kanye West has genuine talent. He has been one of the most popular rappers, besides being a record producer and a fashion designer. Kanye has a very intriguing horoscope. Some sets of planets are extremely powerful and have done their job; some are in the weakest positions and have done some damage. And some events are yet to manifest. Since the weaker planets are more impactful, it looks like there are struggles ahead for Kanye.

---

[112] 'Beyoncé Named Highest-Earning Black Artist of All Time', *MTV*, 29 April 2014, http:// www.mtv.co.uk/beyonce/news/beyonce-named-highestearning-black-artist-of-all-time.

[113] Melissa Stanger, 'How Beyonce and Jay Z Became the World's Top Power Couple', *Business Insider*, 6 December 2015, https://www.businessinsider.in/finance/how-beyonce-and-jay-z-became-the-worlds-top-power-couple/articleshow/50066382.cms.

Kanye's life will resemble a perfect roller-coaster ride. Up and down, up and down again. Kanye conquered his massive debts[114], but it seems he is all set to return to a similar situation.

Kanye has all the four planets—Planet-X, Planet-Y, Planet-Z and Chiron—in strong positions, which makes him a singer, a business person and a famous personality. But even more stronger planets like Uranus and Neptune are debilitated in his horoscope. The positions of these planets made him beg Mark Zuckerberg to invest in his ideas in 2016, as he had a debt of $53 million to repay. He made a great comeback and, by 2019, he was making $150 million a year. This was because the transiting Planet-X was in his favour.

But it is going to be different story in the 2020s. Troubles have already started in his personal life. He divorced his famous wife, Kim Kardashian, in 2021. This is because his Venus is in fall and is in conjunction with Mars, a position inimical to his marital life. But this could just be the beginning of his troubles.

In the 2020s, Uranus will move into his twelfth and first house. Twelfth house represents losses and the first house represents persona. What that would mean is that he can lose money and generally become infamous. Neptune will also transit his tenth house of career, which means that his career will also see a downfall. Pluto transits his eighth house, which can even make him go bankrupt or lose most of his fortune.

If we break up this phase into parts; in the period between 2021-2025, Kanye will return to the phase he went through in 2016, losing money and facing bankruptcy once again. His career will stabilise once again in 2026-2030, when Planet-Z comes back into his third house. His singing career will be resurrected and turn into his saviour. His businesses, too, will start looking up, as Chiron will be in his eleventh house.

---

114   Jade Scipioni, 'Kanye West's Comeback: From $53 Million in Debt to Making Over $150 Million in a Year', *CNBC*, 10 July 2019, https://www.cnbc.com/2019/07/10/kanye-west-from-53-million-in-debt-to-making-millions.html.

At the same time, Uranus in the twelfth house will bring a massive loss during 2025-30. Kanye will encounter troubles again after Uranus enters his first house, reflecting his persona in 2031. His personal brand will take a hit at this time. This time around, the problems will be long-lasting and maybe even permanent.

Prediction # 72

What Does Rihanna's Future Look Like?

Rihanna has the horoscope of a rock star. Her third lord, Planet-X, is exalted in the seventh house, making her a singer. Neptune, the ascendant lord, exalted in the tenth house, makes her an actor and establishes her association with showbiz. Planet-Z in the eighth house, and an exalted Venus in the first, make her a sex symbol.

Neptune will enter her first house of personality, in the 2020s, which will make her even more popular and successful over this decade. Success as a singer, actor and a media professional will continue for her. While her profession will catapult her to greater heights, it seems Rihanna will need a great deal of help in managing her personal life and her investments.

The biggest star of Barbados has her seventh lord, Planet-Y, clearly debilitated, signifying that her personal life and marital life will be a cause for concern. The fifth lord, Chiron, too is debilitated, conveying that all won't be well in her love life either. Love, romance and relationships will be a mirage for her. Rihanna is a person who places a lot of importance on these values, and that's exactly where she will see the biggest ordeals. She hasn't had happy, romantic relationships so far; in fact, she has been in an abusive relationship[115]. She may face more troubles in this area in the future, too.

---

[115] People.com, 'Yes, Chris Brown Remembers Rihanna beating', *Today*, 1 September 2009, https://www.today.com/popculture/yes-chris-brown-remembers-rihanna-beating-wbna32634846.

Rihanna has a big heart. The Aquarius–Pisces combination makes her a good human being and a philanthropist. She has done many charitable concerts and donated huge sums to charity[116]. She has Mercury in Capricorn, which makes her aware of her worth and encash her popularity wisely. It also directs a significant portion of the money to the right causes.

But still, Rihanna can be all heart with her Moon in Pisces, and at times, this can land her in some trouble. Pluto and Uranus being debilitated doesn't help either. During most of the 2020s, Pluto will be transiting her eleventh house that represents business profits in the second half of life. Rihanna is a successful businessperson but she needs to exercise caution in the 2020s. Her wrong decisions will end up losing a lot of her hard-earned money. If the loss is not in her business, her habits or lifestyle could make her fritter away her earnings. Pluto, being the ninth lord could also put her in some legal trouble.

All in all, Rihanna needs a trusted person to handle her money. There could be an interesting twist here. Rihanna may voluntarily decide to donate a major part of her earnings to charity, like Mark Zuckerberg, Bill Gates and Warren Buffett. As long as the outflow of money is voluntary, all is well. Otherwise, she should figure out where she stands, lest she sinks into deep debts.

Prediction #73
What do Katy Perry's Stars Foretell?

Katy Perry's horoscope reveals a multitude of possibilities on both ends of the spectrum—positive and negative. Exalted Neptune in her third house gives her a magical voice. Planet-Z in nascent exaltation in her first house makes her a fab artist. Her fifth lord, Uranus, is exalted, making her a powerhouse in media and entertainment.

---

[116] David Greenwald, 'Taylor Swift Named 2012's Most Charitable Star, Rihanna Gives $1.75 Million', *Billboard*, 26 December 2012, https://www.billboard.com/articles/news/1481248/taylor-swift-named-2012s-most-charitable-star-rihanna-gives-175-million.

However, a few planets in her horoscope are a cause of concern. Her eighth lord, Planet-X, is debilitated in the eleventh house. The eighth house indicates chronic health ailments, and the eleventh house is related to the second half of life and longevity. The eighth house also stands for other people's money, and the eleventh house could mean the returns on that money. Even in the first house, Perry has a debilitated Pluto. The first house reflects the body and the personality.

This has two possibilities. The first possibility, and a less harmful one, is that Katy could have some financial troubles where she could lose money, which might drain her finances or even lead to bankruptcy. The other possibility is that some major health complications could impact the second half of her life.

A weak Pluto's entry into her fourth house of the family will create some real hurdles and disturbances in her family life. Chiron will also be debilitated in her seventh house of marital life and relationships, from 2025 to 2031, indicating upheavals in her associations.

However, Uranus and Neptune will continue to make her sparkle in the world of music. Now, that is good news for Katy.

Prediction #74
Will Suri Cruise Be an Actor?

Suri Cruise has fame in her genes. She was popular even before she was born. She received a lot of attention from the public during her birth, and all through her growing-up years. She will continue to be famous, and the paparazzi will cover her life even in the future. Many aspects of her life will have a resemblance to the lives of her parents.

Suri Cruise is a perfect blend of her famous parents. Her beautiful face is a charming blend of Tom Cruise and Katie Holmes. Astrologically, she is a combination of Aries and Sagittarius, which makes her a stylish actor. Mercury in Pisces also gives her maturity beyond her age. She has the fierce effervescence of her father and the depth of her mother. A strong father is indicated by the exalted Sun. She is blessed with the inheritance of good homes and wealth as conveyed by Uranus in the second house—its own. Planet-X is her fifth lord of fame and popularity, and it is in deepest exaltation in her second house. Planet-Z, her eighth lord, is deeply exalted in her first house of personality. Suri will follow in the footsteps of her famous parents. She will become one of the most popular actors of her time—a phenomenal style icon, an actor par excellence, and also hugely successful. Planet-Z is the natural indicator of arts and showbiz, and it being the eighth lord can make her a great dancer and a sex symbol. Deeply exalted Planet-X in the second indicates that she will also make huge wealth on her own besides a handsome inheritance. Planet-Y in the ninth house shows that she may turn to writing and creative communication. She could even be a popular host in the media.

It seems, though, that Suri has inherited both the positive and negative aspects from her parents. Her third lord Neptune is in debilitation. The third house indicates the mind. A weak third house indicates lots of emotional and psychological hardships. Her seventh lord Chiron is debilitated, and even Saturn is in fall in the seventh house. Problems in the seventh house mean emotional problems arising from love, romance and marriage. It seems Suri will go through lows in love and romance like her parents.

Suri's eleventh lord, Pluto, is also debilitated in her twelfth house, indicating major adversities in the second half of her life. She also needs to be careful with her money management since she might end up with substantial financial losses with some of her ambitious projects going wrong. The planet being Pluto, the scale of losses could be huge, even to the extent of bankruptcy. Will she turn to philanthropy? Possible. If she does that, then the erosion in her wealth would be voluntary and a positive one.

Prediction #75

Can Aryan Emulate His Father?

Papa Shah Rukh Khan (SRK) said that his son Aryan won't join movies as a hero, in an interview with David Letterman[117]. The boy, who has inherited the dashing good looks from his father, reasons that he would always be compared with his father, and he doesn't want to be in that position. Fair point. And yes, it does seem that Aryan may stay away from the limelight indeed.

Aryan Khan has an interesting horoscope. Let us talk about the positive positions first. His Pluto is in its own fourth house of family and Planet-Y in the second house that denotes wealth. Aryan will inherit the business empire from his father, and take it to the next level. His strong Pluto in the fourth house signifies that he will be an astute businessman, enhancing the profits of the existing business and creating a few new opportunities of his own. He will also be an outstanding investor and a fantastic producer due to Planet-Y. Planet-X would be traversing his sixth house in the 2020s, signalling more involvement in the technical aspects of the business than the creative.

Absence of direct planetary connections to the fifth and the seventh houses, indicates that there are fewer chances for Aryan to don the greasepaint and face the camera. He would rather spend time handling production, special effects, or creating more business ventures for his father to invest in. The only consolation for Aryan's Instagram followers would be that he will be associated with the film world somehow or the other. He will be super successful in what he sets out to do—managing the back end of movies and creating new businesses. His biggest career successes in life will come post-2035.

SRK hinted at Aryan's keenness to write, and has declared that he would stay behind the camera. Most good writers and

---

117 Vrutika Shah, '10 Star Kids Who Are Likely to Make Their Bollywood Debut Soon', *GQ*, 16 March 2020 https://www.gqindia.com/entertainment/content/10-bollywood-star-kids-debut-suhana-khan-aryan-khan-ibrahim-ali-khan.

directors have either a strong third house or the ninth. But Aryan doesn't have strong planets in these quadrants to make a career in these fields. Perhaps he won't be going the Salim–Javed way or the Karan Johar way but probably a little bit of everything with particular emphasis on technology.

One worrying factor in Aryan's horoscope is his weak sixth house. The eighth lord, Neptune, is debilitated there along with a debilitated Jupiter. This implies some serious health disorders, which may even be life-altering. The health conditions could be connected to the immune system, blood or may impact some vital organs. But expect Aryan to fight this bravely and overcome the malaise. The other challenge is the placement of a weak Chiron in his third house. Third indicates the mind and hence emotional and psychological difficulties cannot be ruled out either, especially during 2026-2030.

Also, both Aryan Khan's and his sister Suhana's horoscopes reveal some distress for the mother, mostly related to health or personal life.

Prediction #76
How Successful Will Suhana Khan Be?

The daughter of a fashionista mother and an actor father Shah Rukh and Gauri Khan's daughter Suhana inherits fashion and style besides a brilliant gene pool. The birth charts of the sibling predict that there are more chances of Suhana being a film star than her elder brother Aryan.

Planet-Z in nascent exaltation in her first house of personality, promises that she will be a reasonably successful filmstar. She can come close to being as big as Alia Bhatt in the near future. Now Alia is a good actor. Can Suhana match up? To some extent, yes. Suhana doesn't have any water sign in her. Most actors who have exceptional histrionic abilities have either Virgo or other strong water signs like Cancer, Scorpio or Pisces.

Suhana may lack the chameleonic ability of Alia to fit into any character that she plays, but would be a much better actor than most other young girls of her generation. The popularity and the success of her movies can be compared to Alia, though.

Suhana will tick all the boxes necessary and has all the factors working for her to be a successful actor. Suhana's position of Planet-Z, Pluto and Chiron show that she will up the glamour quotient, the oomph factor, and be a fantastic dancer. There will be an interesting amalgamation of honesty, simplicity and sensuality about her which will endear her to fans. The position of deeply exalted Planet-X in her third house can even make her a singer or probably a director/ creative writer at some point of time. And she will find even better success at this. So while Aryan manages the business and technical aspects, Suhana can take care of the creative side of the film businesses.

Interestingly, her horoscope has the strong twelfth house that indicates legs and foreign countries. We are yet to know if Suhana can scorch the dance floor with her moves, but she does have a foreign country connection where she is learning theatre. Probably this international connection can become even stronger in future.

There are two significant hurdles in her horoscope, though. One is the presence of Venus and Mars in conjunction in her chart. This impacts a person's personal life. Venus—Mars conjunction also gives a good exposure to sports and martial arts. Maybe Suhana will face a heartbreak, or she could breaks bones of people, instead! If Suhana does continue her connections with taekwondo and other sports and keeps focus on dancing as well, it will lower the chances of her personal life being impacted adversely. Strange as it may sound, that's how the planets work.

As mentioned earlier, both Suhana and Aryan's horoscopes indicate strong challenges to the mother. Gauri needs to take care of herself besides managing the growing number of stars in her family.

Prediction #77

The Legacy of Donald Trump

Who will lead a life as interesting and as fascinating as Donald Trump himself in Donald Trump's family? Well, it has to be his youngest son, Barron Trump.

Donald Trump has an extraordinary horoscope, which shows his birth in a rich family and inheriting its massive wealth. He was also responsible for the growth and development of the business. Besides, he was also a popular TV-show host and an extremely controversial figure. He went through four bankruptcies in his career,[118] and faced innumerable challenges during his stint as the President of America, including being impeached twice.

Barron's horoscope also promises to be as exciting as his father's. What's life without a few ups and downs—especially if you are a Trump?

Barron has an extraordinary horoscope, with Planet-X in the deepest exaltation in the strongest zodiac sign Aquarius, in his first house. Uranus, too, is in its own house in the first, making it a powerhouse of a horoscope. Planet-X, the fourth lord, being exalted in the first, clearly shows the substantial wealth he will inherit. Besides, he also has Planet-Y in its own house in the eighth, indicating that the young Trump will continue the legacy of real estate and the properties business of the Trumps, and will be a success in them. The placement of Planet-X is exactly the same as Amitabh Bachchan's. Barron could do a Bachchan in his business career. He will be one of the most well-known personalities and make a mark as a tycoon. Curiously, Barron also has his seventh lord Planet-Z in deep exaltation, indicating that he would also have a stint in showbiz and/or politics with success.

---

[118] John Cassidy, 'Donald Trump's Business Failures Were Very Real,' *The New Yorker*, 10 May 2019, https://www.newyorker.com/news/our-columnists/donald-trumps-business-failures-were-very-real.

On the other hand, Barron has Neptune, the second lord, in debilitation in the twelfth house, and his tenth lord, Pluto, in debilitation in the eleventh. The second house indicates wealth, and the twelfth house represents losses. The tenth house denotes career, and the eleventh house shows profits. The weak positions of these planets make this chart very interesting. These placements spell out that Barron may see just as many lows in his career as his father. You could say bankruptcy runs in his genes. He might take some extremely reckless risks in his business that would bomb and probably make him go bankrupt. Exactly like his father.

The good thing about Barron's horoscope is that he will also bounce back strongly, like his father. The clever businessman that Donald is, he let the businesses go bankrupt and didn't accept the blame personally. The younger Trump's horoscope too indicates such incidences. The similarities aren't over yet. Venus in twelfth, Mars in fourth and seventh lord Planet-Z also in twelfth indicate that in terms of relationships, too, the younger Trump will have as colourful a life as his father's.[119]

Barron will ensure the legacy of the Trumps continues. In every possible way!

Prediction #78

The Biggest Bollywood Superstar in the Future

Who is going to be that next big superstar in Bollywood? Will it be a Khan, a Kapoor, a Kumar, or a Roshan? Considering the fact that the star kids have higher chances of at least getting a break in the film industry, let's see who amongst them will make the grade in the future.

---

[119] Kate Taylor, 'Porn Star Stormy Daniels Says She Had an Affair with Trump a Year After He Married Melania', *Busines Insider*, 7 March 2018, https://www.businessinsider. in/politics/porn-star-stormy-daniels-says-she-had-an-affair-with-trump-a-year-after-he-married-melania-heres-a-timeline-of-the-presidents-many-marriages-and-rumored-affairs/ articleshow/63208225.cms.

By the looks of it, the biggest superstar of the 2020s up to the 2040s should be a Kumar. Aryan Khan will not join the race. Ibrahim Ali Khan will shine, Hrehaan and Hridhaan Roshan, will definitely do well. But the person who it seems will tower over all of them will be Aarav Akshay Kumar.

Aarav has got the killer looks. He is the son of one superstar and the grandson of two. Besides looks, he also seems to have inherited talent and the luck factor. Aarav is a Virgo, and hence a perfectionist, naturally—and born to one as well. He has his Sun in Leo, which gives him the style quotient of his father and grandfather. He has his Moon in Sagittarius, making him a good dancer, a fabulous athlete and a natural in front of the camera. Aarav seems to have that elusive combination of good looks and talent. He has the right recipe for success in every way.

Aarav has a fantabulous horoscope—one beyond compare—with an extremely rare arrangement of planets. He has as many as ten planets in strong positions, which indicates the extraordinary life he will lead, and the fantastic successes he will see. Planet-X, the seventh lord in deep exaltation in Aquarius indicates that he will be an actor. Pluto, the most powerful planet in its own house in the ascendant, will make him a huge persona in the industry. All the four asteroids Planet-X, Y, Z and Chiron exalted in the second/fourth/eleventh axis will make him financially hugely successful, not to mention that Uranus in its own house in the fourth is responsible for his birth and lineage. His planets are like a combination of Akshay Kumar and Rajesh Khanna, which is a story in itself.

Will he lag behind in education? Not at all. He will study well. His relationships will make news and keep the gossip mills busy, but he won't be a Casanova. He will be way too focused on his career and success, which he will attain in many ways.

The major challenge in his horoscope is connected to Venus in the twelfth and Neptune being debilitated in the third house. Aarav could go through some emotional challenges and unhappiness due to his relationships.

Aarav will sell brands, newspapers, gossip magazines and set the internet ablaze all by himself. He will be such a fantastic brand and such a film industry leviathan that everyone will want to associate themselves with him. When Aarav carves a niche for himself, his celebrity status and stardom will raise new standards. He can go truly international.

Prediction #79
What Is in Store for Hansika Motwani

She is the Mumbai girl who started as a child artist in Bollywood, and made it big in Kollywood like Khushboo. She even has a temple in her name, just like Khushboo.[120] But there are certain areas of her life which will pan out differently from Khushboo's.

Hansika has an intriguing horoscope, with a mixture of extremely powerful and extremely weak planets in different spheres of life. She has Neptune, her fifth lord, in deep exaltation, which makes her a huge film star. Pluto is in its own house, in the ascendant, making her a sex symbol and a dream girl. Hansika's success story will continue as Neptune enters its own house, her fifth, cementing her position as a mega-star. She will continue to star in some fantastic movies. She may even go behind the camera, with Pluto moving into her third house of communications.

The major handicaps for Hansika stem from her being born on an amavasya day. Her seventh lord, Planet-X, is debilitated, and her Venus and Mars are in conjunction. She will face troubled relationships and marital life. She is destined to go through some painful relationships, and even a divorce.

---

[120] 'A Temple for Hansika Motwani in South', *Lehren Diaries*, 12 August 2019, https://audioboom.com/posts/7339508-a-temple-for-hansika-motwani-in-south.

Her Uranus, the fourth lord, being weak, and being born on amavasya, are not good factors for her gynaecological health. Amavasya-born actresses are associated with some tragedies in life, especially in their personal lives, be it Meena Kumari or Whoopi Goldberg. Hansika needs to be aware of this Achilles heel in her life.

Prediction #80

Something Interesting about the Farah Khan's Kids

Children often inherit a lot of things from their parents. Farah Khan's triplets—Czar, Anya, and Diva—exhibit fascinating aspects and give a peek into the direction that the Farah Khan legacy would take in the future.

All three children have more or less the same horoscope, which means that their lives will be almost identical. They wouldn't be same though, naturally. Their adversities and opportunities will be similar. Uranus is in its own house in the horoscopes—in the twelfth, Planet-Y is in the seventh house; and the third lord, Planet-X, is exalted in the first house. That offers some interesting possibilities.

One thing that comes out strongly is the seventh house, which means that the world of showbiz, media and entertainment will doubtlessly be the destination for these Khan kids. The third house indicates the hands, and the twelfth house indicates the legs. If Farah's children have strong limbs, then the obvious inference is that all the three will be good dancers. Farah Khan had once shared on social media that it had always been her dream to be a ballerina, and that she was living the dream through her daughters.[121] There is no doubt that Anya and Diva will be among the best

---

[121] Less famous star kids: Farah Khan shares a picture of her daughters practising ballet', *E Times*, https://timesofindia.indiatimes.com/entertainment/hindi/bollywood/photo-features/less-famous-star-kids/farah-khan-shares-a-picture-of-her-daughters-practising-ballet/photostory/67773798.cms, accessed 18 March 2021.

ballerinas in the country. As of now, it isn't clear if Czar will dance too. Taking the horoscope into account, it does seem he might—eventually.

What is even more fascinating is that the children also have a strong third house. Farah hasn't disclosed if the children are good at playing musical instruments. One or two of them could. And, again, the third house also indicates the voice. Is there a singer amongst the three? Very likely. Khan & Co. could even make a band of their own, and run a musical show. It is highly possible.

The third house indicates the mind and creativity as well. Planet-X is the third lord and, in the deepest exaltation in the first house, which lends them creativity. For the film industry this could translate into careers connected with creative direction, choreography, singing, playing instruments, dancing, story writing, film direction, music direction and much more.

Farah's kids have a powerhouse of a horoscope. The film industry has been dancing to Farah's tunes. It seems her children's generation may be doing the same with her children. They may or may not choose to come in front of the camera. But Farah has a creative, talented, home-grown team ready, exploring a plethora of creative options in filmmaking and all genres of entertainment. They will be everywhere and will do everything—and be good at all!

Prediction #81

Can Hrehaan Roshan Wear Dad Hrithik's Shoes?

It is amazing how Hrehaan Roshan's life will pan out almost in the same manner as his father's in most aspects of life.

Hrehaan has a powerful eighth house with Uranus, the eighth lord, in its own house. Besides, he also has Planet-X in deep exaltation in the eighth house, making it an extraordinary power centre. Consequently, everything connected with the eighth house becomes enlarged and magnified. Father Hrithik Roshan, too, has a powerful eighth house. The eighth house stands for the physique and the body and physical activity and prowess, especially, dancing skills. Like most sex symbols who have a solid eighth house, Hrithik is no different. Hrehaan's eighth house seems to be even more powerful than his father's with Planet-X in the deepest exaltation in Aquarius.

Hrehaan will work to sculpt his body, like his father. He is bound to be a sex symbol. Besides, he will be one of the best dancers in town. Actors with a strong eighth house also specialise in action roles. Expect Hrehaan to do some adrenaline-pumping daredevil action in movies. Since Planet-X is very powerful, Hrehaan will go on to be a great saleable star, just like his father. His Planet-Z in deep exaltation in the seventh house signals that he will be an actor. And the other planets corroborate that will be phenomenally successful. He will be one of the biggest superstars of his generation, exactly like his father.

Hrehaan also has Planet-Y in its own house—the third. The third house indicates the hands and the voice. Hrehaan could also be additionally interested in martial arts. Don't be surprised if he also picks up the mike and breaks into a song. He will either be a singer–dancer, or a sex symbol–martial artist. Either way he will be super successful in his trade.

Unfortunately, Hrehaan's negative planets seem to be following the pattern of his father's life too. Hrehaan has a fragile seventh house, with Neptune in debilitation and Chiron in fall. His fifth lord, Pluto, is also debilitated in the sixth house. The seventh house shows marriage, marital life and relationships. The fifth house indicates love and romance. The sixth house indicates health. This implies that Hrehaan will go through some excruciating times in his personal life.

A whirlwind, and highly talked about romance and marriage, followed by separation or even divorce can be seen in his chart. Will he choose not to marry at all due to his experiences? That's possible.

Hrithik's physical features may have been inherited by his son. A weak Pluto could also indicate the injuries he might sustain during certain scenes that he would insist upon doing himself. It seems history will repeat itself.

Prediction #82
How Will Beti-B Do in Her Life?

It does seem that there is going to be another superstar in the Bachchan family. And that will be Beti-B, Aaradhya Bachchan. Aaradhya is already a very adorable kid. She dances gracefully,[122] and will only get better with age. Her planets are in Gemini–Libra–Scorpio. Expect her to be a super-smart kid. She will have the fantastic communication skills of a Gemini, the artistic and dancing talents of a Libra, and the intensity, passion and ambition of a Scorpio. She will take to acting like a duck to water—it is in her genes, anyway.

First, let's clear the only hurdle in her life. She has inherited the good looks of the Bachchans and the Rais, as you can see. Her horoscope says that she has also inherited some health problems that run in the family. Her ascendant lord, Pluto, is debilitated, indicating that she will face certain health anxieties. But, like her father and her grandfather, who have braved and overcome personal struggles, Aaradhya too will rise above her physical limitations and perform wonders in her life. The intense Scorpio that she is, like her mother, she will push herself with an iron willpower.

As for the good aspects of her horoscope—there are plenty. Chiron exalted in her fourth house indicates that she was born in a well-known, affluent family. Is she going to be a film actor? Yes, she will certainly be. Will she be a superstar? Yes, she will be an extraordinarily popular superstar. She has planets that suggest a combination of a great actor and a fabulous star.

---

[122] 'Aaradhya Bachchan Dances Like Mother Aishwarya Rai on Stage!!' *YouTube*, 18 May 2019, https://www.youtube.com/watch?v=0CE9Vb_52d0.

Aaradhya has a huge power centre in her fifth house. She has the seventh lord, Planet-X, in deep exaltation in the fifth house of fame, name, showbiz and entertainment. She also has the tenth lord, Planet-Z, of career, in nascent exaltation in the same house. That is simply phenomenal. Think of her as a blend of Smita Patil and Hema Malini in acting skills, fame and popularity, opportunities, and longevity on the screen. Expect her to be a good singer—her third lord, Saturn is exalted, shows she can sing, too. She will be a marvellous dancer, a gorgeous style icon, and an empathetic actress. She will be much more than a beautiful face.

If you come from a film background, you may get the perfect launchpad, but that doesn't necessarily guarantee success. But Aaradhya will tick all the boxes. She will be extremely successful, will star in some of the biggest and the best movies, will launch many brands and go on to be a big brand herself. She has it in her to be the number one actor of her times.

Prediction #83

Children Who Will Follow in Their Parent's Footsteps

Sons of Kareena and Saif

Planet-X is in deep exaltation in the fifth house of Taimur shows that he will certainly join the film industry. Their second son, whose name hasn't been disclosed as of June 2021, has Neptune in its nascent placement in his first house of personality. Neptune embodies showbiz, and he too will be an actor.

Nysa and Yug Devgan

Nysa has at least six planets that indicate she will be in the glamour industry. She is going to sing, dance, romance—and even do daredevil stunts! Yug has Venus and Mars in conjunction and strong sixth and twelfth houses, indicating that he could be doing many angry-young-man roles in *Singham*-style. Yug just needs to mind his temper.

Viaan Raj Kundra/ Azad Rao Khan

It is really amazing that these two star kids born about six months apart have almost similar horoscopes. Both were born exactly at the dawn of the auspicious new moon, and have four planets—Planet-X, Planet-Y, Planet-Z and Chiron—in the strongest positions. Showbiz, media, entertainment, acting, editing, directing, producing—these kids will do it all.

Kabir Kaif

The eighth lord, Chiron, exalted in the third house, suggests that Kabir will be using his arms a lot in his life, most probably in sports, and it seems it will be in cricket.

Agastya Pandya

Agastya, has Pluto, in nascent exaltation in the third house of the hands. Could he be a batsman? Possible. Could he be a bowler? That, too, is possible. Could be he a fast-bowling all-rounder? If Pluto is involved, you can be sure it will be pretty fast bowling.

Vamika

The eighth lord, Pluto, is in nascent exaltation in the tenth house , indicating a career in sports. The eighth house can also mean modelling, or a dance, or a sex symbol—or all three. I would tend to lean more towards a career in the glamour industry.

Izhaan Mirza Malik

The exalted Mars, Planet-X and Planet-Z in the eighth house confirm that he will be a sportsperson. He could make a well-muscled, dancing filmstar too. The first one seems the obvious choice, but we cannot rule out the second either.

Prithvi Ambani

Pluto, the eleventh lord, is in nascent exaltation in the first house. The fifth lord, the god of wealth itself, Planet-X, is in its own house. The second lord of wealth, Uranus, is exalted in the fourth house, of the family. What that means, if you are an Indian, is that you will continue to buy many more products from the Ambanis for years to come.

Siddharth Roncon

Siddharth is a footballer and a sprinter[123]. Interestingly, Uranus and deeply exalted Planet-X are in his fifth house. Siddharth's uncle and his grandparents were actors. I wouldn't be surprised if, one day, Siddharth decides to pursue the glamour world instead of sports. And if he indeed sticks to sports, he will achieve enough fame that rivals a movie star's.

Prediction # 84

The Next Male Superstars in the 2020s

Who is a superstar? I would say an actor with a fan following across age groups. People flock to cinema halls for their movies but their star value doesn't depend on the success of their previous movie , or their exceptional acting skills. And they have starred in some milestone movies that have raked in big bucks most of the time . Amitabh Bachchan, Shah Rukh Khan, Salman Khan, Rajinikanth and Hrithik Roshan are prominent examples.

Here are my predictions of potential male superstars. This list consists of some who have already established themselves as stars, and even those trying to find their feet in the industry.

---

[123] Joe Williams, 'After Actors & Politicians, an Athlete in Dutt's Family', *The Free Press Journal*, 23 August 2019 https://www.freepressjournal.in/sports/after-actors-politicians-an-athlete-in-dutts-family.

Ayushmann Khurrana

Ayushmann is already a legend in small-budget films. He has Jupiter, Saturn, Uranus, Neptune and Planet-Z in super-strong positions, underlining his status as the king of movies with good stories. But can he be a superstar? No, not possible. Pluto, in debilitation in his horoscope, will prevent him from achieving that iconic status.

Vicky Kaushal

He is another talented actor with the chameleonic ability to blend into the character he is portraying. This new-moon born actor, with Neptune in exaltation, will stand out for some time. But being a superstar is not really possible as he has Uranus and Pluto, two major planets, in debilitation.

Rajkummar Rao

Rajkummar was born just a few days apart from Ayushmann Khurrana and has a very similar chart. He can aspire to be another Ayushmann, but nothing beyond that.

Ahan Shetty

Suniel Shetty's son, Ahan, has Pluto in its own house and Planet-X in exaltation. Though these are good placements, to be an actor of some repute, one needs to have more planets in either deep or nascent exaltation. Ahan has none of these qualifications.

Ishaan Khattar

Ishaan is an upcoming actor who has been lauded as a promising talent. He has Neptune and Planet-X exalted, and Pluto in its own house, which will enable him to do well as an actor. As none of the planets are in deep or nascent exaltation, he will miss superstardom.

Kartik Aaryan

He had a slow start to his career but has had a couple of hits and is suddenly hot property. Kartik's appeal doesn't really transcend the age factor, but it seems he will get there slowly as Pluto and Neptune will favour him now onwards, in the 2020s. Therefore, Kartik has chances of becoming a superstar over some time.

Siddhant Chaturvedi

He has made a huge impact with the supporting role as MC Sher in *Gully Boy*. He has Pluto in nascent entry into its own house. He has Neptune and Planet-X in deep exaltation, Chiron in its own house, and the Sun, Jupiter and Venus in exaltation. That is a phenomenal horoscope. He was born just a month apart from Alia Bhatt and, if Alia can be called a superstar, then Siddhant, with the same planets in similar positions, will also make it in due course. He is the one!

Prediction # 85

The Next Female Superstars in the 2020s

Janhvi Kapoor

Pluto and Planet-X are in strong positions in Janhvi's horoscope, one of which has given her a privileged birth and the other which will help her remain an actor for some years. But superstardom—that's very far away.

Ananya Pandey

Ananya has Pluto in the ascendant, which makes her an actor. Ananya has Neptune debilitated in her birth chart, and it will be transiting her fifth house, of popularity, in the 2020s, which shows that she may not get the kind of success expected of her. Interestingly, she has a deeply exalted Planet-X in her third house which can give her brilliant successes behind the camera, like a creative writer or a director.

Manushi Chillar

Pluto, the strongest planet in her horoscope, is in its own house, in the twelfth, and that's what made Manushi a Miss World. But all the Miss Worlds and Miss Universes who have gone beyond and achieved even bigger success in showbiz, had more planets in stronger positions connected with the fifth and the seventh houses specifically. The absence of such configurations in Manushi's horoscope will make her go the Yukta Mookhey and Diana Hayden way. But she wouldn't be able to make it big in the film industry, definitely not as a superstar.

Sara Ali Khan

Sara has a good horoscope, with exalted Neptune, Chiron and Pluto in their own houses. None of the planets are deeply exalted, but the arrangement is good enough for her to have good longevity in the industry. She won't replace Deepika Padukone but will undoubtedly make a name for herself.

Tara Sutaria

With Planet-X, Neptune and Chiron in exaltation and Pluto in its own house, Tara has the best chance to excel in the industry. She will do some memorable roles, and will generally have outstanding longevity as Planet-X is in nascent exaltation in her birth chart. Tara's horoscope undeniably looks the best amongst all the youngsters discussed so far.

Malavika Mohanan

Malavika does have a fabulous horoscope. She has Planet-Z and Neptune, two of the most important planets connected to showbiz, in deep exaltation and Pluto, too, in nascent entry into its own house. She has acted in a handful of South Indian movies and will make her debut in Bollywood in 2021. What a year to debut! Malavika suddenly looks like a good horse to bet on.

Unlike the men's list, where we could identify a possible superstar, the women's list doesn't throw up a clear winner. Malavika and Tara are in the same age bracket as the current superstar Alia Bhatt who was born in 1993. The next superstar girl would be born in the early 2000s. She isn't visible now. Or have we discussed her horoscope in another chapter without realising that she is the one? Possibly.

Prediction #86

Celebrities Who Need to Mind Their Health and Body

Lewis Hamilton

Lewis Hamilton has got his eighth lord Planet-X in debilitation in his eleventh, Chiron debilitated in eighth and Pluto in debilitation in his ascendant. For a sports person, it can mean injuries and physical harm, but the number of planets and their magnitude makes it worrying.

Infanta Leonar

Infanta's seventh house of royalty has deeply exalted Planet-X and Uranus in its own house, signifying very clearly that she will become the Queen one day.

Unfortunately for her, her eighth lord, Neptune, is in debilitation in the sixth house, indicating some serious health troubles. This could be connected to the immune system, or it can even involve some internal organs or blood. Gynaecological problems cannot be ruled out either.

Emma Watson

The main hurdle in her horoscope is the position of the Sun and Mercury in the eighth house. Additionally, Venus and Mars are in conjunction in the sixth, and even the sixth lord Uranus is in debilitation. Some nagging health problems can impact and weaken her body. The weak eighth house can even point towards any untoward incidents or accidents that can cause her bodily harm.

Renee Zellweger

Renee Zellweger, a recipient of numerous accolades, including two Academy Awards, has a fragile eighth house and sixth house. Her eighth house contains debilitated Chiron, and the eighth lord Neptune itself is debilitated. Saturn, her sixth lord and her ascendant lord Planet-Z are debilitated too. A weak Neptune would be traversing her eighth house in the 2020s and is an ominous sign for the beautiful actress.

Michael Phelps

A sickly child with dyslexia went on to become the greatest Olympian of all times. Beat that! He also had suicidal thoughts after winning the Olympics. Most of his hardships come from Planet-X's debilitation in his third house of the mind.

Michael has his sixth lord Pluto in debilitation, transiting his eighth house in the 2020s. This could mean he may go through some serious health complications, both mental and physical. Unfortunately, it seems Michael's miseries aren't over yet.

Tyler, The Creator

Tyler, The Creator, a famous rapper, has his eighth lord, Uranus, in debilitation in his sixth house. Tyler also has the Sun and Mercury in the eighth house, which is not a good indication of his health. There could be health issues connected to the immune system or lifestyle. This can lead to some serious repercussions. Tyler needs to manage his health better.

Elle Fanning

Elle needs to manage her health as her eighth lord, Planet-Z, is in deep debilitation in her eleventh house. This can lead to some serious problems in health even before she turns fifty.

In her twenties and thirties she also needs to be careful about psychological issues as Neptune, her debilitated planet, would be traversing her third house of the mind.

Nayanthara
The weakest planet of her horoscope is Pluto, which is in a Grey Lizard position in her chart. During the 2020s to 2030s, Pluto will be transiting her eighth house. Being the sixth lord of health, transiting the eighth house of chronic health isn't a good sign and requires the heartthrob of millions to take good care of her health.

Rana Daggubati
There are two significant challenging positions. He has Planet-X in debilitation in the eighth house. A debilitated Pluto will enter his first house of personality, in 2020 and remain there for the next 17 years. Can excessive focus on bodybuilding take a toll? Maybe. Or is it something else that we will discover when it unfolds? It will be something that will impact his name, fame and popularity in some way and/or impact the body.

Sunidhi Chauhan
Planet-X, her eighth lord, is debilitated in the eleventh house. Her eleventh lord, Planet-Z, is also debilitated in the twelfth house, which doesn't really augur well for the second half of her life. The 8–11–12 connections of Planet-X, Planet Y and Chiron point to worrying factors connected to her health.

Prediction #87
Celebrities Who Need to Mind Their Minds
Pluto transited into Capricorn during the fag end of 2019 and will remain there for almost two decades. During this phase, people with the Scorpio ascendant will have the mighty

planet traversing their third house of the mind. A similar thing would happen with people having a Capricorn ascendant and a debilitated Neptune in their birth horoscope. Neptune would be strong now and will be an opposing force.

The third house represents the entire psychological make-up of a person. Everything that affects the emotions is a part of the third house. People who have positive transits to the third house would do well emotionally, and their happiness quotient would be high. But negative transits to the third house can be devastating. It will disturb the mental, psychological and emotional balance of the person. While it can cause worries and emotional disbalances in some, it can lead to clinical depression in others, and it can even lead to psychological diseases like Alzheimer's, especially if it reflects in the horoscope.

Let us look at some famous people who will go through negative transits to their third house.

Scarlett Johansson

Pluto is in the deepest debilitation in her twelfth house and will be traversing her third house during the 2020s. The third house indicates the mind, and the Tony Award winner runs the risk of going through some of the lowest emotional moments during this period. The planet Uranus will also remain debilitated between 2024–2030 in her seventh house, clearly revealing that all will not be well in her personal and marital life too. Scarlett was born with amavasya in her first house of personality and the body. So emotional lows and psychological troubles will impact her body and her career too. Scarlett needs to be careful about her mental and emotional health.

Mila Kunis

A debilitated Pluto will be traversing the third house of the Ukraine-born American actress. A debilitated Chiron in the seventh house says this could affect her relationships too. Mila and her spouse Ashton Kutcher need to work together to help Mila overcome some huge emotional and psychological distress.

Tiffany Trump

Her fourth lord Neptune is exalted in her first house, indicating a privileged birth. She has an amavasya indicating her parents' divorce and as many as ten planets in weak positions, signalling the various challenges she will see in her life. The worst position is her third lord Uranus in debilitation in her ascendant and a debilitated Saturn in her third house. The third house of the 'mind' is significantly damaged. This means that Tiffany would go through various issues which will impact her sanity. Most of the troubles are in the area of relationships. This heiress needs help to prevent herself from being a wreck.

***

A few other famous personalities who will have Pluto traversing in the third house in a negative position in the 2020s are:

Cheryl Cole, Naomi Campbell, Tori Spelling, Sean Penn, Nikki Sixx, Nadia Comaneci, Vincent Lindon, Ian Somerhalder, Russell Brand, Charlotte Gainsbourg and Alicia Silverstone.

Prediction #88
Huge Challenges for Some
Pippa Middleton

Pippa has dabbled as an author and a columnist, besides being a well-known socialite. Pippa was born on amavasya day , besides having her Mars in the twelfth house. Planet-X, her tenth lord, is also debilitated in her ascendant. She also has a debilitated Planet-Z in her second house of wealth. This doesn't augur well for the sister of the Princess of Wales.

Her career as an author may not take off. While her career as a fashionista would be promising, she will not do exceptionally well. Pippa should be cautious as she may end up investing in some wrong businesses and even lose a lot of money.

She has married James Matthews, a hedge fund manager and heir to a 10,000-acre estate in Scotland. She has the title of Lady Glen Affric. After 2024, there will be considerable difficulties in her marital life and family because of the transit of Uranus and Pluto in negative positions. Pippa also needs to mind her health as Pluto is transiting the sixth house of health. The amavasya in her first house can even tarnish her image for some reason or the other.

Kylie Jenner

Kylie Jenner was listed as the youngest self-made billionaire even before the *Forbes* magazine showed how the data related to her businesses was manipulated to promote her. She comes from the wealthy Jenner family, so the 'self-made' tag doesn't fit her. Her horoscope shows a major set of planets causing a huge downfall to her. The second lord has a debilitated Neptune, and the eleventh house has a debilitated Chiron showing that her wealth may go down. Even the twelfth house of losses, contains the Planet-Z, which implies that she will have a famous downfall.

Noor Pahlavi

Noor Pahlavi was born after her father was exiled to America. She has a fantastic horoscope, indicating a great life. There are only three blots in her horoscope. The eighth lord Uranus is debilitated in her sixth house, which points to significant health issues. Her Mars is in the eighth house, and Saturn in the seventh, indicating huge troubles in her marital life. Finally, the eleventh lord, Planet-X, is in debilitation, suggesting that she would be infamous for some wrongdoings in her later part of life.

Victoria, Crown Princess of Sweden

Princess Victoria, the heir-apparent to the Swedish throne, has an unfortunately weak horoscope. Planet-X is exalted in her seventh house, making her a royal, and the seventh lord Chiron itself is exalted in the fifth , which would even make her a queen. But the rest of the planets show that there could be a tragic story that would unfold. She has an amavasya in the sixth house of health, which represents the numerous health problems she has been through. She has dyslexia, anorexia and an eating disorder. Her eighth lord, Planet-Z, is debilitated. She also has Uranus debilitated in her eleventh house, revealing the dangers to her body, mind and life.

Prediction #89

All is Not Well in Their Paradise

Jake Gyllenhaal

Jake hasn't been very lucky in relationships so far. He has dated Kirsten Dunst and Taylor Swift and hasn't yet settled into a stable relationship. A debilitated Pluto, the lord of his fifth house of love and romance could be blamed for this. Unfortunately for Gyllenhaal, Pluto will be traversing his seventh house of marriage and relationships from the 2020s to 2030s, and so the worst is not over yet for the handsome actor.

Zendaya

Zendaya seems very sorted despite huge popularity at a young age. Zendaya, unfortunately, has the combination of Venus and Mars in the seventh house of relationships. More importantly, her third lord, Neptune, is in debilitation in her first house. The third house indicates the mind and it seems that she will go through some really difficult moments due to her mental issues, which could be caused by her relationships.

Miley Cyrus

She announced her split from Cody Simpson in August 2020, after ten months of dating. Miley has a fragile seventh house. She has amavasya in the seventh house and as many as six planets in the house indicate huge struggles in her love life. Venus and Mars are in undesirable positions, so she will have hindrances in her love life even in the next two decades.

Benedict Cumberbatch

This versatile and fine actor has a good horoscope connected to his profession. But the weakest planet in his horoscope is Neptune, which is his seventh lord of marriage. Neptune is debilitated in his horoscope and will traverse his seventh house during the 2020s, predicting a turbulent marital life. His Mars in the twelfth house doesn't help either.

Marion Cotillard

Marion is a Cancer–Virgo–Libra. Even if she goes through the most challenging issues, she will cling to the relationship and stretch herself to make it work—she will never give up. Marion will be subjected to multiple tests of her resolution during the 2020s when her seventh lord, Uranus, will remain weak.

Gerard Butler

Gerard Butler, a Scottish actor and producer, would have his debilitated Neptune traversing his seventh house in the 2020s. He split from his wife of seven years, Morgan Brown, in 2020. But it seems the bad luck connected to relationships wouldn't be over soon for the handsome actor.

***

Pixie Lott, Ewan McGregor, Laetitia Casta, Javier Bardem, Diane Kruger, Asia Argento, Guillaume Canet and Chris Martin have weak planetary transits in their seventh houses during the

2020s. They will all have severe hardships in the area of love, romance and relationships.

Dwayne Johnson, Shannen Doherty, Ice Cube and Billy Corgan are some famous American celebrities who have weak Neptune in their horoscopes and will have Neptune traversing their seventh house of marriage, in the 2020s. All of them will face huge adversities in their marital life. They could also have some disputes in a business partnership or with the law. Their life partners could also face some troubles.

Prediction #90

Celebrity Couples Who Will Face Challenges in Their Relationships

Blake Lively and Ryan Reynolds

They make a cute couple, and their fans wish they remain together forever. But it seems the most powerful planets in the universe—Neptune and Pluto—won't allow them. Blake will have a debilitated Pluto transiting her seventh house of marriage, and Ryan will have a debilitated Neptune transiting his seventh house of marriage in the 2020s. Venus and Mars are in conjunction in the horoscope of Blake, for whom this is the first marriage. This couple will have to make considerable efforts to remain together.

Emily Blunt and John Krasinski

John has amavasya is in his sixth house , of health. His eleventh lord, Neptune, who affects the second half of life, is debilitated in his seventh house of marriage. Emily has Venus and Mars in conjunction in her chart, besides her seventh lord Pluto being debilitated. Pluto will be traversing her ninth house of luck, which means that she will turn unlucky in love. Looking at John's horoscope, it appears that some difficult circumstances will force them apart—something over which both of them will have no control, something which may be tragic and more like an act of fate.

Tom Brady & Gisele Bundchen

One of the greatest quarterbacks of American football has had a long, fifteen-year relationship with his supermodel wife, Gisele Bundchen. The couple admitted that they have had many issues in their relationships and as recent as 2020 too but have worked hard on these challenges. The 2021–2025 period will bring in fresh challenges to this beautiful couple. A debilitated Neptune is entering the seventh house of Tom Brady, and the seventh lord of Gisele, Chiron, is already debilitated. The next half-a-decade will be a testing time for them to stay together. For Gisele, as Chiron is traversing the third house, it can lead to huge emotional breakdowns. The couple needs to sort out a lot of things together.

***

Elon Musk and Grimes (Claire Elise Boucher)
Ryan Gosling and Eva Mendes
Justin Bieber and Hailey Baldwin Bieber
Orlando Bloom and Katy Perry
Karlie Kloss & Joshua Kushner

These couples also have problematic seventh houses, and Venus and Mars in troubled positions. They will go through hardships in their relationships.

Prediction #91
Celebrities Who Run the Risk of Infamy

If you are a celebrity, then you always run that one risk; one can become infamous too. An uncommon person can be infamous too. But when one is famous, the stakes of being infamous is very high. The planet that is assigned specifically to 'fame' is Planet-Z. When Planet-Z is in an exalted position and the right house, a person can achieve glory, successes and colossal victories in whatever they do. Popularity, brand endorsements, recognition, awards and rewards, popularity in the media follows. The fifth house stands for everything that can be used to describe the Planet-Z—name, fame, popularity, rewards, everything.

It gets interesting when Planet-Z is debilitated, especially in a famous person's chart in the fifth house. There is a very high possibility that the person would be infamous at some point in time. The fifth house also indicates a lack of recognition for the work one has done. The fifth house also signals challenges connected with children. Moreover the fifth is also the house for love and romance. So, the placement of Planet-Z has to be carefully evaluated. Now, a strong possibility of a person becoming infamous arises when the Planet-Z debilitated in the fifth house is the ruler of the eleventh house. The eleventh house indicates the latter part of life, especially above 45 years of age. Most of the time, problems connected with love, romance, children and recognition would have been over by then. Often a person who has not been through the manifestations of any of these troubles in early life, before 45 years, can become particularly vulnerable to becoming infamous in the second half of life.

Some celebrities who had this position include Jeffrey Epstein, Harvey Weinstein, Bertrand Cantat, Kamal Haasan (his out-of-wedlock children created negative criticism in the 1980s).

Besides, it is not just about Planet-Z. But any higher hierarchy planet being the fifth lord debilitated in the ascendant can also give infamy. Also, any higher hierarchy planets being debilitated in the fifth can be a cause for infamy. Salman Khan, Lance Armstrong, Hrithik Roshan, Julian Assange, Winona Ryder are examples of such placements.

Let us look at some of the celebrities who run this risk. They apparently haven't been through such events before. They need to safeguard themselves against any such incidents and be aware of the risks and traps in their lives which can lead to infamy.

Celebrities with fifth lord Neptune debilitated in the ascendant.

Jude Law
Bradley Cooper
Will.I.am
Michael Fassbender
Matthias Schoenaerts
Celebrities with eleventh lord Uranus in fall in fifth
Patrick Dempsey
Elle MacPherson
Celebrities with eleventh lord Planet-X in fall in fifth
Selena Gomez
Nick Jonas
Rita Ora
Shailene Woodley
Louis Ducruet
Celebrities with seventh lord Neptune in debilitation in fifth
Brooklyn Beckham
Romeo Beckham
Prince Michael Jackson II
Prince Hisahito of Akishino
Maisa Silva
Celebrities with Planet-Z debilitated in fifth
Ashton Kutcher
John Krasinski

Pluto is Not a Planet?
Are You Kidding?

I developed an instant dislike to the author Mike Brown when I saw the title of his book, *How I Killed Pluto and Why It had it Coming*. It smacked arrogance and condescension. This astronomer and professor has, what appears to me, a rather distasteful social media profile called @plutokiller! Yes, he has Leo for a moon sign and the pride shows. My dear friend, you have only killed the status of the body, not the body itself.

Unfortunately, he may never know or realise the gravity of his error. Brown was born in 1965, an important year astrologically, as you know by now. Strange, isn't it, that a man who has Pluto in deep exaltation in his horoscope chose to topple it from its position as a planet? Can there be greater irony? And when was this done? In 2006, when Pluto just went into debilitation. More than Brown doing it to Pluto, the planet did it to itself. Brown may never realise that he was born to do just that.

Astronomers name a celestial body, based on its shape, size, orbital path, and some other parameters they deem fit, to put the body into a certain category. In astrology, we name the body based on its impact on human beings and the events it can cause. While astronomy, the physical classification of heavenly bodies and their movements, is recognised as a science, astrology, the study of the impact of the movements upon human life and the events of the world, isn't. Not yet.

Regardless of whatever the astronomers may say, my simple endeavour is to show you that Pluto is indeed a planet. In fact, it took me decades of research to add a few more bodies to the list of 'planets', which may never be considered as such by the astronomers of the world but, in astrological parlance, will still be. Pluto can never be killed! On the contrary, it is the one that kills, or changes, or transforms things permanently.

Scholars of physics may disagree with metaphysics. This book tries to show that certain things are intangible and don't fall clearly into black and white categories. Many mysteries in this world are beyond human comprehension. Explaining life itself is one such thing. Astrology is one such tool available to decipher life. I firmly believe it is a science, with every rule in the science book applicable to it. Hopefully, someday in the future, the powers will realise this and encourage and fund more outstanding research in the field. In fact, there is enough evidence to show that astrology precedes even astronomy as a discipline. It is now time that astrology regains its past glory. Pluto will certainly help re-establish that.

Acknowledgements

Fingers on the keyboard don't often keep pace with one's thoughts. And, by the time you've finished writing a sentence, you have forgotten the next one. The online dictation.io was a huge time saver and, thanks to it, I could finish writing the chapters in this book on time and faster.

I thank all my friends, relatives, colleagues, and students who came up with their set of questions. I have tried to cover the maximum I could in this book.

Thank you, Derek, once again for the contacts for the accurate birth data I needed.

Thank you very much, Divya Dubey, for helping me with the initial editing of the manuscript. The questions you posed helped me shape the book to its current form. Your inputs at every juncture helped me gain a better understanding of the reader's perspective.

While Divya ensured that the words I used were appropriate and the language correct, Sanjiv Sareen ensured that data, facts, history, references were correct and relevant to context. Thank you, Sanjiv.

I had the best kind of editors for my work.

I had the luxury of choosing the book cover from among six great designs. Thanks, Saurabh Garge, for those brilliant cover options.

Vidhi Bhargava, you were the super editor, psychologist,

coordinator and friend—who was always there to ensure that everything went right. The book has appeared in its current avatar due to your timely interventions—from conception to the final product. A special thanks to you!

Greenstone Lobo
June, 2021